D0935688

# Selected Sonnets

# *Luís de Camões* SELECTED SONNETS

Edited and Translated by William Baer

*The University of Chicago Press*
CHICAGO AND LONDON

WILLIAM BAER is editor of *The Formalist* and professor of English at the University of Evansville. He is the author of two books of poems, most recently *"Borges" and Other Sonnets,* and editor of three books of interviews, most recently *Elia Kazan.*

The University of Chicago Press, Chicago 60637
The University of Chicago Press, Ltd., London

Printed in the United States of America

14 13 12 11 10 09 08 07 06 05     1 2 3 4 5

ISBN: 0-226-09266-6 (cloth)

Library of Congress Cataloging-in-Publication Data
Camões, Luís de, 1524?–1580.
[Sonnets. English & Portuguese. Selections]
Selected sonnets / Luís de Camões ; translations by William Baer. — Bilingual ed.
p. cm.
Includes bibliographical references and index.
ISBN 0-226-09266-6 (cloth : alk. paper)
1. Camäes, Luâs de, 1524?–1580 —Translations into English. 2. Sonnets, Portuguese. 3. Sonnets, Portuguese—Translations into English. I. Baer, William, 1948– II. Title.
PQ9199 .A5 2005
869.1'2—dc22

2004058521

♾The paper used in this publication meets the minimum requirements of the American National Standard for Information Sciences—Permanence of Paper for Printed Library Materials, ANSI Z39.48–1992.

With it Camöens soothed an exile's grief . . .

"SCORN NOT THE SONNET" WORDSWORTH

# Contents

# Illustrations

LVIS D̃
CAMÕ
ES

# Introduction

Luís de Camões (1524–80), the greatest of Portuguese writers, has been described by Harold Bloom as the "transcendent genius of his nation." Camões is the author of the last great Western epic, *Os Lusíadas,* and he was also one of the most sublime lyric poets of the Renaissance, often compared to Dante, Petrarch, and Shakespeare. The poet's life, as commentator Henry H. Hart remarks, is "so fascinating and adventurous that it borders on the unbelievable." The young Camões, a regular at the Lisbon court, lost an eye fighting the Moors in Morocco and was later arrested for stabbing a royal favorite in a Lisbon street brawl during the Corpus Christi celebrations of 1552. He was subsequently banished to the Eastern empire where he fought in several military engagements, served as a government official in Macao, China, and was charged with embezzlement.

Recalled to India, Camões, by his own account in *Os Lusíadas,* was shipwrecked off the Cambodian coast and survived by swimming to shore clutching the only manuscript of his epic-in-progress. Subsequently, he was jailed in Goa, India, for his activities in Macao and his unpaid debts. After seventeen years in the East, Camões found himself stranded in abject poverty in Mozambique. When he was fortuitously rescued by several friends, he was finally able to return to Lisbon, where he published his national epic, *Os Lusíadas,* six years before the disastrous death of King Sebastião and his Portuguese army at Alcácer-Kebir in Morocco.

Camões died in Lisbon in 1580 during an outbreak of the plague, just before Spain seized his beloved Portugal. Luís de Camões led a truly amazing life, one that Henry H. Hart has aptly described as "more adventuresome by far than that of François Villon, as chivalrous as the *Cyrano de Bergerac* of Edmond Rostand, and as replete with excitement, love, and tragedy as *The Three Musketeers* of Alexandre Dumas."

## *The Life*

As is the case with his younger contemporary, Shakespeare, only a few indisputable facts concerning Camões's life can be verified by the public record. He lived in an era before the archivally useful habit of keeping personal diaries, and once Camões became famous, the "facts" of his life became enmeshed in a fascinating but frustrating web of legend, speculation, and pure invention. But despite these mythologies, there's much that we do know for certain.

Luís de Camões, according to an entry in the records of the Casa da India, was born in 1524, the son of Simão Vaz de Camões and Ana de Sá. He was from an impoverished but well-connected family that had originally come from Galicia in Spain when his ancestor, Vasco Pires de Camões (a minor poet), moved to Portugal in 1370 to serve under King Ferdinand I. On his mother's side, Luís was a distant kinsman of the legendary Vasco da Gama, who would eventually serve as the central figure in Camões's *Os Lusíadas.* It seems most probable that the young Luís de Camões grew up in Lisbon and, given his extraordinary erudition, it's also reasonable to assume that he studied at the renowned University of Coimbra, founded in 1290. It's clear from his writings, especially his lovely sonnet about the Mondego River, that Camões indeed spent time in Coimbra.

Sometime in the early 1540s, Camões returned to Lisbon. He was often at court and writing poetry, but he was also a bit of a young swashbuckler, keeping company with a group of rowdy friends. During this period, according to legend and numerous biographers, Camões reputedly fell in love with Caterina de Ataide, a young lady at court who would become the inspiration for much of his love poetry. There's been a long debate as to whether Caterina de Ataide was really Camões's "Beatrice," and some commentators have suggested instead the Infanta Dona Maria and others. Nevertheless, the case for Caterina is the most compelling, especially given Camões's lyrics that refer to a beloved "Natercia," an anagram for "Caterina."

Whether it's true that his love for Caterina was disapproved of by the Crown and that he was subsequently shunted off to military exile is much more debatable. Nevertheless, it's certain that in 1547 Camões, as a common soldier, joined the garrison in Ceuta, Morocco, where he would lose his left eye fighting against the Moors. By June 1552, Camões was back in Lisbon, where he was arrested after a street brawl during the celebrations on the feast of Corpus Christi. During the altercation, he inflicted a sword wound on a minor court official named Gonçalo Borges, who survived his injury. As a result, Camões was incarcerated in Tronco prison, paid a fine, and was eventually shipped out as a common soldier to India. He sailed on the *São Bento,* the only ship of four to arrive safely in Goa, India, that year. Over the next three years, Camões was involved in a number of military engagements, including action on the shores of Malabar, as well as the Straits of Mecca and the East African coast.

In 1556, with his military obligation completed, Camões was appointed the Trustee for the Dead and Absent in Macao, China. In this not insignificant position, Camões was responsible for the maintenance of all the properties of those abroad and deceased. It was an opportunity for Camões to finally make his fortune, and he seems to have done quite well until the charges of malfeasance, which he claims in *Os Lusíadas* (canto X, stanza 128 ) were totally "unjust." Summarily dismissed from his position and recalled to

Goa to answer for his actions, Camões, as he vividly describes in the epic's same passage, lost all his material possessions in a devastating shipwreck near the mouth of the Mekong River off Cambodia. Only his strong swimming skills allowed him to survive, and to bring with him through the waves and currents of the ocean his sole copy of *Os Lusíadas* and, presumably, his lyrics as well.

When Camões finally arrived in Goa, he was jailed for his alleged embezzlements. Eventually the charges against him were dismissed, but his impoverished situation landed him back in jail when he couldn't pay his debts. From his writings, it's very clear that Camões never liked the important trading city of Goa, which was the hub of the great Portuguese empire in the East, and which Camões, in one of his few surviving letters, called "the mother of knaves and the stepmother of honest men." His continual despair in Goa ("Babylon") and his longing for Lisbon ("Zion") is a constant and powerful theme in his lyric poetry.

Eventually, Camões managed to arrange passage to Mozambique in 1567, but he ended up stranded and penniless on the African coast. When he was finally discovered by the Portuguese historian Diogo do Couto and another friend, they were appalled by his condition, and they gave him the necessary money to complete his passage back to Lisbon on the *Santa Clara.* When, at long last, Camões arrived back in his beloved country, Lisbon was engulfed in the plague, and the country itself was absorbed with the grandiose ambitions of its young king, Sebastião. As for Camões, after seventeen years abroad, he'd returned to his native land even poorer than when he'd left. At the age of fifty-one, his only publication thus far had been a dedicatory poem for Garcia da Orta's *Colóquios dos simples e drogas e cousas medicinais da India, etc.* (Goa, 1563), a scientific book about medicinal plants. His beloved Caterina de Ataide had long been dead (1556), and he'd returned to Portugal an obvious failure. The world had seemingly passed him by. All he had were his manuscripts.

Two years later, in 1572, Camões published his epic poem, *Os Lusíadas,* in Lisbon with the approval of the ecclesiastical censor. The book, dedicated to King Sebastião, is a paean to the Portuguese people and an account of the history-making journey of Vasco da Gama in 1497–98. The book was very well-received and apparently popular at all levels of Portuguese society. King Sebastião, gratified by the tribute, awarded the poet a modest but most welcome pension. Six years later, the young king led his troops into Africa, and his army was obliterated by the superior Muslim forces at Alcácer-Kebir. Not only was Sebastião killed, but the entire flower of the Portuguese nobility perished in the distant deserts of Morocco. It was the most devastating moment in the history of the valiant Portuguese nation; and it seemed so incomprehensible to the people in Portugal that the great myth of the king's survival and his forthcoming return ("Sebastianism") forced itself into the cultural consciousness of the nation; and it still, in various manifestations, survives today. The impact of Alcácer-Kebir on Camões, the poetic chronicler of Portuguese history, was devastating. Not long before his death two years later in 1580 during a revival of the plague, Camões wrote a friend in one of his few extant letters: "I have come to the end of my life, and everyone can see that I loved my native land so much that I was content to die not only in it, but with it."

Having returned to his Catholic faith, Camões died in the arms of the Dominican Frei Josepe Indio, who later reported that the famous poet died in poverty, without even a burial shroud (*Luiz de Camões,* 1923). As Camões had requested, his remains were interred in the nearby Church of Santa Ana. There was no coffin, and his body was placed in an underground crypt along with many other coffinless victims of the plague. Later that same year, after a Spanish military force had invaded Portugal, King Philip II arrived in Lisbon to claim the Portuguese throne and initiate sixty years of Portuguese subservience to the Spanish crown. On his arrival,

Philip, who'd previously read *Os Lusíadas,* is reputed to have asked for Camões. When he learned that the great poet had died, he was sorely grieved, and it's clear from the royal records that he permitted Camões's elderly mother to continue receiving the poet's pension until her death.

Thus the legend of Camões was clearly underway, but his lyrics, among the most beautiful in world history, were still unknown and unpublished.

## *Camões's Literary Work*

While Camões made his living as a professional soldier and a public official, his true and obsessive vocation was as a writer of verse, which he composed over three tempestuous decades. Despite the disorder of his writing career, his literary achievements fall rather neatly into three categories: the epic, the lyrics, and the plays.

### THE EPIC

Camões's international reputation was initially based on his authorship of the last great Western epic, *Os Lusíadas,* published in 1572, eight years before his death. It's clear that the project consumed much of his life. Most scholars agree that he probably conceived the idea of a national epic long before he left Lisbon in 1553, and that his extraordinary experiences in the Orient inspired him to focus the poem on the epoch-making journey of the Portuguese admiral Vasco da Gama, who sailed to India around the Cape of Good Hope in 1497. Contemporary Americans rightly recognize the history-making voyage of Christopher Columbus to the Americas in 1492, but at the end of the fifteenth century, Europe was much more interested in the gradual progress of the Portuguese navigators around Africa, culminating in the voyage of Camões's

distant kinsman five years later. Da Gama's voyage opened up the trade lanes to the Orient and initiated an incredible Portuguese trading empire that would soon span more than half the globe, from the Amazon to the Moluccas in Indonesia. The impact of da

Gama's accomplishment on world history is staggering and, for modern minds, it's often compared to the endless potentials and ramifications of the *Apollo 11* moon landing on July 20, 1969.

But Camões's *Os Lusíadas* not only chronicles the adventures of da Gama's journey, it also exalts the vision and bravery of the Portuguese people and their entire history. Camões, while writing his epic a half century after da Gama's journey, is literally living within the Eastern empire which it created. He's also writing at a time when the resources of the small Portuguese nation were being severely strained in its efforts to maintain its vast trading empire, especially given Spanish, English, and Dutch incursions. There's a clear sense in his epic, as well as in his lyrics, that Camões is living in a time of Portuguese decline, and his natural patriotism and his wariness of his country's enemies, especially its Islamic enemies, inspire him to remind his Portuguese contemporaries of their heroic past.

*Os Lusíadas* is a masterfully crafted poem in 1,102 ottava rima stanzas, divided into ten sections (cantos) which depict the progression of da Gama's journey. As with his sonnets, in which Camões begins with the model of Petrarch, in *Os Lusíadas* the poet similarly uses Virgil's *Aeneid* as his initial model and then quickly extrapolates into a remarkable originality, most famously: the murder of Inês de Castro by King Afonso's henchmen on the banks of the Mondego in 1355; the conjuring of the Titan sea god, Adamaster; the poetic descriptions of St. Elmo's fire and the waterspout; and Venus's creation of the "Island of Love" for the triumphant Portuguese sailors. Despite the centrality of the figure of Vasco da Gama and Camões's obvious admiration for the great adventurer, it's important to note that the poem is really about the Portuguese people as a whole, as its title, *Os Lusíadas (The Portuguese),* makes clear. Upon its publication in 1572, Camões's extraordinary literary accomplishment was quickly recognized in Portugal, the entire Iberian peninsula, and subsequently across Europe. In *Don Quixote*

(1605), Cervantes, one of the many admirers of *Os Lusíadas,* rightly calls Camões "the incomparable treasure of Lusus."

### THE LYRICS

In the appendix to his 1884 translations of Camões's lyrics, Sir Richard Burton reminds his readers of the Portuguese truism, "If Camões had not written his *Lusiads,* Portugal would have had a Petrarch." The international reputation of *Os Lusíadas* and the fact that Camões's lyrics were published posthumously have often left the latter underappreciated, even though they are generally regarded by both poets and scholars as among the best of the Renaissance lyrics. Certainly Camões took them seriously, beginning with the early love poems that he wrote as a young man at the Lisbon court and then later those documenting his emotional and intellectual vicissitudes during his long sojourn in the East. As with *Os Lusíadas,* Camões's lyrics reveal him as a master craftsman, writing sonnets (discussed below), odes, elegies, eclogues, and *redondilhas* with equal skill and with a deep emotional impact. The scholar J. D. M. Ford expresses a common contention when he points out that even if Camões had never written his famous epic, his "flawlessly crafted sonnets and lyrics would have won him lasting fame."

### THE PLAYS

Camões produced three comedies in verse which were published posthumously, although they may have had occasional local performances during his lifetime. *Filodemo* recounts a medieval love story; *Rei Seleuch* recasts Plutarch's famous love story about the Syrian King Seleucus; and *Amphitryões* is a loose adaptation from Plautus. All of these plays have their literary distinctions, and they are now considered superior to the other Portuguese plays of their time. But they had little impact, given their posthumous publica-

RHYTHMAS
DE LVIS DE CAMOES.
Diuididas em cinco partes.

*Dirigidas ao muito Illustre senhor D. Gonçalo Coutinho.*

*Impressas com licença do supremo Conselho da geral Inquisição, & Ordinario.*
EM LISBOA,
Por Manoel de Lyra, Anno de M. D. Lxxxxv.
A custa de Esteuão Lopez mercador de libros.

tion, on either contemporary Portuguese drama or European drama, and, whatever their merits, they clearly suffer in comparison with the poet's lyrics and his legendary epic.

## *The Sonnets*

The distinguished Argentine poet J. L. Borges, who once wrote a sonnet of tribute to Camões, also wrote a sonnet titled "Un poeta del siglo XIII" ("A Poet of the Thirteenth Century"), which speculates about the creation of the very first sonnet. The poem claims that the form of the original sonnet was a divine gift from the god Apollo to an anonymous Italian poet of the 1200s. Borges describes this extraordinary gift as "un ávido cristal" ("a greedy crystal") that attracts and reveals anything and everything. Certainly Borges is right about the power and the endless capabilities of the sonnet format. Born in the late middle ages, the fourteen-lined sonnet is one of the greatest human artistic creations, and its early perfections by Dante and Petrarch and its subsequent history in a wide range of languages and national literatures bear this out. Camões, like the other Renaissance poets who followed Petrarch's lead (Garcilaso, du Bellay, Ronsard, Shakespeare, etc.), clearly recognized the powerful potential of the little *soneto*, and, over the course of his lifetime, he created a remarkable corpus of unforgettable sonnets.

As with Petrarch and Shakespeare, many of Camões's finest lyrics are love poems, and his sonnet "Alma minha gentil, que te partiste . . ." ("Dear Gentle Soul") is one of the most famous in Iberian history. Nevertheless, long before the English poets ever attempted to expand the thematic parameters of the sonnet, Camões was writing brilliant sonnets about a wide range of topics: nature, history, historical figures, classical mythology, biblical subjects, patriotism, religion, and even contemporary Portuguese politics. Yet whatever his subject, the trait that most distinguishes Camões's sonnets is the undeniable and tangible presence of the writer himself. Camões's poems about love, or despair, or human corruption are never simply poetic abstractions on a theme. Underneath all of Camões's poems is the palpable presence of Camões himself, often suffering, always struggling, always exposed and fully human. Few poets of any period in history have been able to create such an emotional exposure of the suffering, individual self. In conjunction with this sympathetic presence, there is also the constant air of sorrow in Camões's poems, what the Portuguese describe as *saudade.* Although Camões's sonnets were not the first literary portrayals of Portuguese *saudade,* they expressed the melancholic condition in a way that still has a powerful effect on readers from any culture.

## *Camões's Influence and Reputation*

Immediately after the publication of *Os Lusíadas* in 1572, Camões was recognized as a great poet in his native land and in neighboring Spain. Even in Italy, his distinguished contemporary, the poet Torquato Tasso, called Camões the "prince of poets," and the Italian also wrote a famous untitled sonnet about da Gama and Camões in 1580, the year of Camões's death. According to Sir Richard Burton, Tasso admitted that he "feared no man but Camoens" as a poetic rival. As mentioned earlier, Cervantes similarly praised Camões as "the incomparable treasure of Lusus" in his *Don Quixote* (1605). Other continental admirers of Camões were Lope de Vega, Goethe, and even Voltaire, who referred to him as the "Portuguese Virgil" in his *La Henriade* (1723).

The first translation of *Os Lusíadas* into English was published by Sir Richard Fanshawe in 1655, and the second appeared over a hundred years later in William Julius Mickle's influential couplet version of 1776. As for the lyrics, Philip Ayres published a translation of one of Camões's sonnets in 1687, but it was the literary commentator William Hayley, in his 1782 *An Essay on Epic Poetry; in Five Epistles,* who first brought Camões's lyrics to the attention of English readers. Hayley had the highest praise for Camões's sonnets, and he translated one himself. The first ambitious translation of Camões's lyrics into English appeared in Lord Viscount Strangford's *Poems, from the Portuguese of Luis de Camoens; with Remarks on his Writings, Notes, &c.* (1803) which inspired among the English Romantics a deep appreciation of the Portuguese "Petrarch." Byron was a great admirer; Southey translated a number of the poems; and Wordsworth, in his famous "Scorn Not the Sonnet," defends the sonnet by citing Petrarch, Tasso, Camões (whose use of the sonnet "soothed an exile's grief"), Dante, Spenser, and Milton. Of course, the greatest tribute to Camões came at midcentury from Elizabeth Barrett Browning, who not only wrote the famous poem "Caterina to Camoens," but then titled her sonnet sequence *Sonnets from the Portuguese* (1850), pretending that the intimate love sonnets that she'd written during her courtship to Robert Browning were actually translations from Portuguese sonnets in the Camonian tradition.

In America, Camões was similarly admired by Edgar Allan Poe; Hawthorne, who included Camões's work in several anthologies; Emily Dickinson, who knew his poetry through the influence of Thomas Wentworth Higginson; and, most significantly, Herman Melville. It's hardly surprising that the poet-sailor author of *Moby-Dick* (1851) would have a lifelong fascination with Camões. His deep appreciation expressed itself in various ways, especially in his novel *White Jacket* (1850), in which the sympathetic sea captain, Jack Chase, is a great admirer of Camões, and also in Melville's uncollected, but subsequently well-known, two-part poem, "Camoens" and "Camoens in the Hospital."

Later in the nineteenth century, the Englishman J. J. Aubertin published his translation of *Seventy Sonnets of Camoens* (1881), and three years later his friend Sir Richard Burton translated the *Lyricks of Camoens* (1884). These editions were very well received and again increased Camões's reputation as a sonneteer. This popularity is made clear by the title of a subsequent book of translations by Richard Garnett entitled *Dante, Petrarch, Camoens: CXXIV Sonnets* which appeared in 1896. Thus by the end of the 1800s, Camões's reputation as both a lyric and epic poet was firmly established. As the Portuguese poet and critic Jorge de Sena described it in 1974: "At the end of the nineteenth century, Camões was thought to be the Renaissance poet and man par excellence, after having been for the European Romantics a paragon of the adventurous genius who lives unhappy in love and dies a miser [in misery] ignored by society" (*Trinta Anos de Camões,* 1980).

Although there have been numerous new translations of *Os Lusíadas* in the twentieth century, Camões's sonnets have yet to be given their due. Henry H. Hart included a number of prose renderings from the lyrics in his book *Luis de Camoëns and the Epic of the Lusiads* (1962). Jonathan Griffin translated fourteen of the sonnets for *Camões: Some Poems* (1976), and Keith Bosley translated twenty sonnets for L. C. Taylor's *Luís de Camões: Epic and Lyric* (1990). The present volume is the first book in over a hundred years (since Burton in 1884) to translate a sizable selection of the poet's sonnets. Nevertheless, despite the chaos of the twentieth century, many distinguished modern poets have not forgotten Camões. Roy Campbell in his 1946 collection, *Talking Bronco,* wrote a dedicatory sonnet to the Portuguese author which concludes:

He shouldered high his voluntary Cross,
Wrestled his hardships into forms of beauty,
And taught his gorgon destinies to sing.

Similarly, Elizabeth Bishop, who lived much of her life in Brazil, was a great admirer of Camões, and J. L. Borges, who recognized his Portuguese ancestors in his sonnet "Los Borges" (one can't help wondering if the great Argentine was descended from the Borges whom Camões stabbed during the brawl in Lisbon), also wrote another sonnet "A Luis de Camoens" which ends with the sestet:

Quiero saber si aquende la ribera
Última comprendiste humildemente
Que todo lo perdido, el Occidente

Y el Oriente, el acero y la bandera,
Perduraría (ajeno a toda humana
Mutación) en tu Eneida lusitana.

which translates poetically:

So I wonder if you ever understood,
before you crossed that final shore to final rest,
that everything which seemed lost and gone for good—
your sword, your flag, the Orient, and the West—
would resurrect, free from the human curse
of change, in *Os Lusíadas,* your epic verse.

## *The Portuguese Sources*

In 1595, fifteen years after the poet's death, Camões's friend Gonçalo do Coutinho decided to arrange for the publication of the poet's lyrics. The resulting *Rhythmas de Luís de Camões* (Lisbon, Editio Princeps) was a small quarto that appeared later that year and contained 171 various lyrics, including sixty-five sonnets, a number of which proved to have been written by other authors. This little quarto initiated a long and convoluted series of subsequent publications of the lyrics in which each new edition contained additional but sometimes wrongly attributed poems. The ever-increasing stature of Camões, both in Portugal and abroad, led overzealous editors to assign countless debatable new lyrics to the corpus of their beloved national hero. A brief and superficial summary indicates the problem: the second issue of the *Rhythmas* (1598) added 43 sonnets; a so-called Second Part *Editio* (1616), edited by Domingos Fernandes, added 41 sonnets; a subsequent Third Part, entitled *Rimas* (1668), edited by Álvares da Cunha, added 91 more sonnets; the multi-volumed *Rimas Várias,* edited by Manuel de Faria e Sousa (1685, 1689), added 67 new sonnets; the *Obras* (1720) of J. Lopes Ferreira added 38 more; and the famous *Obras* (1860–69) of Viscount Juromenha added another 34. Thus Camões's sonnet total increased from 65 in the first edition to over 350 in later editions. Many of these poetic attributions were correct, but many were not. Some came from unidentified sources, some were taken from the anonymous Portuguese "songbooks," and a significant number were taken from the work of Diogo Bernardes (1530–1605?), a talented Portuguese poet who was one of the few survivors of Sebastião's disaster at Alcácer-Kebir.

Modern scholars, following the lead of Friedrich Wilhelm Storck in his important biography of the poet, *Luis de Camoens Leben* (1890), have raised serious questions about the many reckless attributions to the Camonian canon. Important work has been done by Jorge de Sena, Cleonice Berardinelli, Leodegário A. de Azevedo Filho, and many others (see bibliography); and, although there are still many debates about specific attributions that will never be resolved, most modern scholars generally assign about 200 to 250 sonnets to Camões's extant authorship. The best modern editions of the lyrics are Álvaro J. da Costa Pimpão's *Rimas* (revised edition, 1973), which includes 166 sonnets; Cleonice Serôa da Motta Berandinelli's *Sonetos de Camões: corpus dos sonetos Camonianos* (1980), which includes 400 sonnets; and Maria de Lurdes Saraiva's *Luís de Camões Lírica Completa, Sonetos,* Volume Two (1980), which includes 366 sonnets, of which the editor considers at least 215 to be authentically Camonian. For the purposes of the present volume, I have translated only those sonnets which are generally undisputed, with three exceptions, which are discussed in the notes. Similarly, as with Shakespeare and all the Renaissance poets, there are occasional textual variants regarding the sonnets, and I have generally followed the *Sonetos* of Maria de Lurdes Saraiva while citing significant textual deviations or problems in the notes.

## *The Translations*

Luís de Camões was obsessed with the sonnet, and he spent much of his lifetime expressing his deepest thoughts in beautifully crafted *sonetos.* Given this fact, I have done my best to render Camões's sonnets as sonnets, both in form and content. Camões always wrote his sonnets in the Italianate format, and the rhyme schemes of his octaves never varied *(abbaabba)* although he used a variety of formats for his sestets (mostly *cdecde, cdcdcd, and cdedce).* With few exceptions, I have kept his exact rhyme schemes in the sestets and, given the limited number of four-sound rhymes in English, I have used the more flexible *abbacddc* in the octaves. As expected, Camões's sonnets are metrically tight, although his rhythms are smooth and melodic, so I have used the versatile English iambic pentameter for his decasyllabics. Although there is something to be said for "literal" prose translations, which are especially useful to the scholar and student, I have tried to render Camões's sonnets in the exacting form he loved and to which he dedicated his life. Doing so has led to some aesthetic liberties, but my primary objective in all these poems has been to render, as best I could, what Helen Vendler in her essay "Camões the Sonneteer" describes as Camões's "exploration of the most obscure reaches of human consciousness," and to try, with English meters and rhymes, to highlight with sound, as his originals do so beautifully, Camões's poetic "explorations."

Unfortunately, it is impossible, with few exceptions, to date Camões's poems with any useful accuracy. Sir Richard Burton, in the appendix to his translations of 1884, claimed that establishing the dates of Camões's compositions would be as "unsatisfactory and arbitrary as the task of chronologising the *Koran.*" Given this situation, I have presented the poems in this collection in no specific order, but I have, nevertheless, tried to give a sense of Camões's wide variety within a general progression from his more youthful love lyrics, to the increasing *saudade* of his sojourn in the Orient, to his eventual return to Lisbon and his Roman Catholic faith. Also, in the typical Renaissance manner, virtually all of Camões's original sonnets were untitled, but given that it's the convention of our own times to use titles, I have added English titles to the translations. I feel it's appropriate for this selection of translations, the first extensive rendering of the sonnets in over a hundred years, and I hope it will be helpful to the reader, especially since this edition is bilingual, and the original untitled texts are conveniently *en face.* It's been a daunting task to attempt to translate the lyrics of a legend like Camões, especially in rhymed and metrical sonnets, but it has been a privilege to serve him as well as I can.

Of course, no book like this could be completed without assistance. I'm most grateful to Professor Jonas Barros of the Universidade Metodista de Piraciaba, São Paulo, Brasil, for his assistance in the production of these translations. We went over every line of these sonnets together, and I greatly appreciate his attention to detail, his interpretive insights, and his patience. I'm also indebted to Randolph Petilos of the University of Chicago Press, and to the press's two anonymous reviewers, who offered both encouragement and invaluable suggestions. I'm similarly grateful to all the literary editors who published selections of these translations in their various periodicals. I'd also like to thank my generous readers, Carolina Cuervo Grajales, Mike Carson, Rob Griffith, and Paul Bone, as well as the University of Evansville for its helpful ART and ARSAF Grants. Finally, I'm forever grateful to the U.S. Fulbright Commission which arranged for my year-long lectureship at the University of Coimbra, where I fell under the spell of the generous Portuguese people and the legendary works of their brilliant poet, Luís de Camões.

*William Baer*

# Chronology

1524 Born, probably in Lisbon, the only child of Simão Vaz de Camões and Ana de Sá Camões.

c. 1540 Assumed to be studying at the University of Coimbra in the late 1530s and early 1540s.

c. 1543–46 An associate at the royal court of King João III in Lisbon.

1544 Allegedly sees Dona Caterina de Ataide, a young noblewoman, at Good Friday Mass on April 13th and falls passionately in love.

1547 During his much-debated "exile" from Lisbon, sees action as a common soldier at the military garrison in Ceuta, Morocco, and loses his left eye.

1549 Returns to Lisbon.

1550 Registers for a passage to India but never sails.

1552 Arrested for stabbing Gonçalo Borges, a minor court official, in a street brawl during the Corpus Christi celebrations in June. Incarcerated in Tronco prison, he eventually pays a fine and is sent to India as a common soldier.

1553 Sails in March for India on the *São Bento* and arrives safely in Goa.

1553–56 Involved in various military expeditions on the Malabar coast, the Red Sea, the Straits of Mecca, and the coast of East Africa.

1556 Appointed Trustee for the Dead and Absent in Macao, China. Visits Malacca and the Moluccas on the journey to Macao. Caterina de Ataide dies in Lisbon.

1559 Charged with embezzlement, stripped of his position, and ordered back to Goa. Then shipwrecked at the mouth of the

Mekong River off Cambodia, swimming to shore clutching the manuscript of his epic poem, *Os Lusíadas.*

1561–67 Jailed in Goa until the charges are dismissed. Then jailed again for failure to repay his debts.

1563 His dedicatory poem is published in Garcia da Orta's *Colóquios dos simples e drogas e cousas medicinais da India, etc.,* a study of medicinal plants. His first publication.

1567 Secures passage to Mozambique, trying to get home to Portugal, but ends up stranded on the African coast.

1569 Discovered living in abject poverty by two friends, Diogo de Couto and Heitor de Silveira. With financial assistance from his friends, he sails for Lisbon on the *Santa Clara.*

1570 Arrives in Lisbon after seventeen years in the Eastern empire. The capital city is wracked with plague.

1572 Publishes *Os Lusíadas* with a dedication to the young King Sebastião. Awarded a small pension.

1576 His sonnet, "Vós, Ninfas da gangética espessura . . . ," appears in Pêro de Magalhães Gândavo's *História da Província de Santa Cruz a que vulgarmente chamam Brasil,* a history of Brazil. It's the only Camonian sonnet published in his lifetime.

1578 The disastrous defeat of King Sebastião and his Portuguese army at Alcácer-Kebir in Morocco. Eight thousand perish along with the young monarch, and 15,000 are captured and enslaved by the Moroccan Muslims.

1580 Dies June 10 in Lisbon, unmarried and without known issue, attended by the Dominican Frei Josepe Indio. Buried without a coffin in the nearby Church of Santa Ana. Soon after, the Spanish King Philip II invades Portugal and claims the Portuguese crown. Portugal becomes a vassal state of the Spanish monarchy for the next sixty years.

1595 *Rhythmas de Luís de Camões,* the first publication of Camões's lyrics, appears in Lisbon.

1598 Publication of the expanded second edition of *Rhythmas.*

# Selected Sonnets

*O dia em que eu naci moura e pereça . . .*

---

O dia em que eu naci moura e pereça,
não o queira jamais o tempo dar;
não torne mais ao mundo e, se tornar,
eclipse nesse passo o Sol padeça.
A luz lhe falte, o Sol se lhe escureça,
mostre o mundo sinais de se acabar;
naçam-lhe monstros, sangue chova o ar,
a mãe ao próprio filho não conheça.
As pessoas pasmadas, de ignorantes,
as lágrimas no rosto, a côr perdida,
cuidem que o mundo já se destruiu.
Ó gente temerosa, não te espantes,
que este dia deitou ao mundo a vida
mais desventurada que se viu!

# Curse

Wipe away, with death, the day of my birth;
may it be forgotten forever, and never
come back in the sweep of time. And if it ever
returns, eclipse the sun and blacken the earth.
Let all light fade and disappear. Let wild
omens reveal that everything must die.
Let monsters be born. Let blood rain from the sky.
Let every mother not recognize her child.
Let all the stunned and terrified people, with tears
streaking down their faces, pale and worn,
believe their world is doomed and overthrown.
You, frightened people, accept these wonders and fears,
for this was the wretched day on which was born
the most miserable life that ever was known.

---

Como quando do mar tempestuoso
o marinheiro, lasso e trabalhado,
de um naufrágio cruel já salvo a nado,
só ouvir falar nele o faz medroso,
e jura que, em que veja bonançoso
o violento mar e sossegado,
não entre nele mais, mas vai, forçado
pelo muito interesse cobiçoso;
assi, Senhora, eu, que da tormenta
de vossa vista fujo, pro salvar-me,
jurando de não mais em outra ver-me:
minha alma, que de vós nunca se ausenta,
dá-me por preço ver-vos, faz tornar-me
donde fugi tão perto de perder-me.

## Shipwreck

Like the weary sailor, the refugee
from wreck and storm, who escapes half-dead,
and then, in terror, shudders with dread
at the very mention of the name of the "sea";
who swears he'll never sail again, who raves
he'll stay at home, even on the calmest days,
but then, in time, forgets his fearful ways,
and seeks, again, his fortune above the waves;
I, too, have barely escaped the storms that revolve
around you, my love, traveling far away,
vowing to avoid another catastrophe,
but I can't, the thought of you breaks my resolve,
and so, I return to where, on that fateful day,
I nearly drowned in your tempestuous sea.

---

Enquanto quis Fortuna que tivesse
esperança de algum contentamento,
o gosto de um suave pensamento
me fez que seus efeitos escrevesse.
Porém, temendo Amor que aviso desse
minha escritura a algum juízo isento,
escureceu-me o engenho co tormento,
para que seus enganos não dissesse.
Ó vós, que Amor obriga a ser sujeitos
a diversas vontades! Quando lerdes
num breve livro casos tão diversos,
verdades puras são, e não defeitos . . .
E sabei que, segundo o amor tiverdes,
tereis o entendimento de meus versos.

# Reader

As long as Fortune dangled in my sight
the hope of happiness, my wishful schemes
for lasting love and all my youthful dreams
compelled me to lift my pen and write.
But Love, afraid I might prove indiscreet
and reveal her unpleasant truth, ingeniously
obscured my mind and cruelly tormented me,
trying to keep my pen from exposing her deceit.
But *you,* whom Love has also subjugated
to her fickle will, if you should come across
my verses, this little book of diverse
songs, conceived in experience, created
in truth, remember: the more you've loved and lost,
the better you'll comprehend my verse.

*Brandas águas do Tejo . . .*

---

Brandas águas do Tejo que, passando
por estes verdes campos que regais,
plantas, ervas, e flores e animais,
pastores, ninfas ides alegrando;
não sei (ah, doces águas!), não sei quando
vos tornarei a ver; que mágoas tais,
vendo como vos deixo, me causais
que de tornar já vou desconfiando.
Ordenou o Destino, desejoso
de converter meus gostos em pesares,
partida que me vai custando tanto.
Saüdoso de vós, dele queixoso,
encherei de suspiros outros ares,
turbarei outras águas com meu pranto.

# Tagus

Gentle waters of the Tagus, you flow
across the fields, nourishing the herds,
the blooming plants, the flowers, and the birds,
delighting the nymphs and shepherds as you go.
Sweet waters of the Tagus, I don't know when
I'll ever be able to come back home to you,
and, anxiously, before I say adieu,
I begin to doubt if I'll ever return again.
Destiny, intent on finding a way
to turn my joys to sorrows, now commands
this difficult parting, full of regrets and fears.
Still longing for you, and complaining, I sail away,
to breathe my sighs in the airs of foreign lands,
disturbing distant waters with my tears.

---

Por cima destas águas, forte e firme,
irei por onde as sortes ordenaram,
pois por cima de quantas me choraram
aqueles claros olhos pude vir-me.
Já chegado era o fim de despedir-me,
já mil impedimentos se acabaram,
quando rios de amor se atravessaram
a me impedir o passo de partir-me.
Passei-os eu com ânimo obstinado,
com que a morte forçada e gloriosa
faz o vencido já desesperado.
Em que figura ou gesto desusado
pode já fazer medo a morte irosa,
a quem tem a seus pés rendido e atado?

# Tears

Over these waters I sail to whatever lies
ahead, to whatever the Fates desire, since I've
already, somehow, managed to survive
the watery tears that fell from my lover's eyes.
It was time to leave: a thousand troubles were,
at last, overcome on that sad departure day,
but then her streams of love obstructed my way,
trying to keep me from sailing away from her.
But with obstinate will, I passed through her tears,
like one, already doomed, who calmly foresees
his death with the fearless despair of certain defeat.
So how, when angry, ravenous Death appears,
will he attempt to frighten me, when he's
finally got me bound and prostrate at his feet?

---

Os vestidos Elisa revolvia
que lhe Eneias deixara por memória:
doces despojos da passada glória,
doces, quando seu Fado o consentia.
Entre eles a fermosa espada via
que instrumento foi da triste história;
e, como quem de si tinha a vitória,
falando só com ela, assi dezia:
«Fermosa e nova espada, se ficaste
só para executares os enganos
de quem te quis deixar, em minha vida,
sabe que tu comigo te enganaste;
que, para me tirar de tantos danos,
sobeja-me a tristeza da partida».

# Dido

Dido looks at her lovely dresses, the proud
memories Aeneas has left behind, the sweet
remains of their once-and-faded glory—"sweet,"
at least, for as long as the fickle Fates allowed.
Among these things, she finds his custom-made
and beautiful sword, an instrument that reeks
with death. And yet, strangely confident, she speaks
directly to the sharp and shimmering blade:
"Beautiful Dardan sword, if you assume
that you've been left behind to execute
the deceitful desires of the one who loved me, then fled,
be aware: it's only a vanity to presume
that you're needed to end my life, his resolute
betrayal is more than enough to leave me dead."

---

Vós, Ninfas da gangética espessura,
cantai suavemente, em voz sonora,
um grande Capitão, que a roxa Aurora
dos filhos defendeu da noite escura.
Ajuntou-se a caterva negra e dura,
que na áurea Quersoneso afouta mora,
para lançar do caro ninho fóra
aqueles que mais podem que a ventura.
Mas um forte Leão, com pouca gente,
a multidão tão fera como nécia
destruindo castiga e torna fraca.
Pois, ó Ninfas, cantai; que claramente
mais do que fez Leónidas em Grécia,
o nobre Leonis fez em Malaca.

## For Leonis Pereira

Nymphs of the Ganges jungle sing sweet and light
yet vibrantly of that mighty captain whom
the purple goddess, Dawn, has saved from doom,
helping him survive the sons of the darkest night.
The Achém king had amassed his mob of possessed
and wild Malaccan natives, determined to drive
Leonis from his fortress, dead or alive,
along with his bold warriors from the west.
But the mighty lion attacked the mob, though severely
outnumbered, with his loyal Portuguese,
leaving his enemy destroyed—and weaker than ever before.
So all you lovely nymphs, sing out clearly:
since even more than Leonidas did in Greece,
the noble Leonis did on the Malaccan shore.

---

A fermosura desta fresca serra
e a sombra dos verdes castanheiros,
o manso caminhar destes ribeiros,
donde toda a tristeza se desterra;
o rouco som do mar, a estranha terra,
o esconder do sol pelos outeiros,
o recolher dos gados derradeiros,
das nuvens pelo ar a branda guerra;
enfim, tudo o que a rara natureza
com tanta variedade nos of'rece,
me está, se não te vejo, magoando.
Sem ti, tudo me enoja e me avorrece;
sem ti, perpetuamente estou passando,
nas mores alegrias, mór tristeza.

## Nature

The beauty of the sweet, fresh mountains here,
the shade of the green chestnut trees, the pace
of all the gently crawling streams, this place
where all one's sadness seems to disappear.
The hoarse sounds of the sea, the lands that lie
below, the sun hiding near the hills, the last
of the lingering cattle slowly moving past,
the clouds still gently warring in the sky.
But, finally, all these beauties of nature, pouring
forth their various splendors, only create
harsh fresh wounds since you're not here with me.
Without you, everything is disgusting, and boring;
without you, I feel, even within this great
natural happiness, the greatest possible misery.

---

Quando o sol encoberto vai mostrando
ao mundo a luz quieta e duvidosa,
ao longo de ũa praia deleitosa,
vou na minha inimiga imaginando.
Aqui a vi os cabelos concertando;
ali, co a mão na face, tão fermosa;
aqui, falando alegre, ali cuidosa;
agora estando queda, agora andando.
Aqui esteve sentada, ali me viu,
erguendo aqueles olhos tão isentos;
aqui movida um pouco, ali segura;
aqui se entristeceu, ali se riu . . .
enfim, nestes cansados pensamentos,
passo esta vida vã, que sempre dura.

## On the Beach

As the hazy sun, caught in the clouds above,
casts its light over the world below,
I wander this beach, in the gentle, muted glow
of the sun, thinking of the lady I love.
Sometimes, over there, I watched her combing
her hair, and over there, I saw her touch her face.
Sometimes she worried, but mostly she spoke with grace
and charm—sometimes standing, sometimes roaming
the beach; sometimes, sitting right there, she'd gaze
at me, raising her gentle luminescent
eyes—often content, sometimes in pain,
or sadness, although, at other times, she'd amaze
me with her laugh. So now, caught in all these incessant
dreams, I waste away my life in vain.

---

Amor é um fogo que arde sem se ver,
é ferida que dói, e não se sente;
é um contentamento descontente,
é dor que desatina sem doer.
É um não querer mais que bem querer;
é um andar solitário entre a gente;
é nunca contentar-se de contente;
é um cuidar que ganha em se perder.
É querer estar preso por vontade;
é servir a quem vence o vencedor;
é ter, com quem nos mata, lealdade.
Mas como causar pode seu favor
nos corações humanos amizade,
se tão contrário a si é o mesmo Amor?

# Amor

Love is a fire that burns, but is never seen;
a wound that hurts, but is never perceived;
a pleasure that starts a pain that's unrelieved;
a pain that maddens without any pain; a serene
desire for nothing, but wishing her only the best;
a lonely passage through the crowd; the resentment
of never being content with one's contentment;
a caring that gains only when losing; an obsessed
desire to be bound, for love, in jail;
a capitulation to the one you've conquered yourself;
a devotion to your own assassin every single day.
So how can Love conform, without fail,
every captive human heart, if Love itself
is so contradictory in every possible way?

---

Ditoso seja aquele que somente
se queixa de amorosas esquivanças;
pois por elas não perde as esperanças
de poder n'algum tempo ser contente.
Ditoso seja quem, estando absente,
não sente mais que a pena das lembranças;
porque inda que se tema de mudanças,
menos se teme a dor quando se sente.
Ditoso seja, enfim, qualquer estado
onde enganos, desprezos e isenção
trazem o coração atormentado.
Mas triste quem se sente magoado
de erros em que não pode haver perdão,
sem ficar n'alma a mágoa do pecado.

## Sin

Happy is he whose only problem worth
complaining about is love's audacious schemes,
since they alone can never destroy his dreams
of finding some contentment here on earth.
Happy is he who, far from home, embraces
nothing but his long-lost memories,
because when new problems arise, he sees
them clearly, comprehending the sorrow he faces.
And happy is he who lives in *any* state
where only fraud and love's deceits and doubt,
are able to torture his heart from within.
But tragic is he who lives beneath the weight
of some unforgivable act, living without
consciousness of the damage of his sin.

*Triste, pois me não vale o sofrimento . . .*

---

Ditosas almas, que ambas juntamente
ao céu de Vénus e de Amor voastes,
onde um bem que tão breve cá lograstes
estais logrando agora eternamente.
Aquele estado vosso tão contente,
que só por durar pouco triste achastes,
por outro mais contente já o trocastes,
onde sem sobressalto o bem se sente.
Triste de quem cá vive tão cercado,
na amorosa fineza, de um tormento
que a glória lhe perturba mais crescida!
Triste, pois me não vale o sofrimento,
e Amor, pera mais dano, me tem dado
pera tão duro mal, tão larga vida!

# Dead Lovers

Happy young lovers, who've ascended together
into the heavens of Venus and of Love,
where joys, so brief on earth, will now, above
this world, endure forever and forever.
Your happy hours on earth, once undermined
only by their vexing brevity,
are now exchanged for a perfect peace that's free
from all disruptions and fears of any kind.
But sad is he, who lives on earth in vain,
still trapped in love's entanglement, whose grief
increases with love and its inexorable strife.
Sad am I, for my pain brings no relief,
and Love, just to intensify my pain
and wound me more, prolongs my useless life.

---

Correm turvas as águas deste rio,
qua as do céu e as do monte as enturbaram;
os campos florecidos se secaram,
intratável se fez o vale, e frio.
Passou o verão, passou o ardente estio,
ũas cousas por outras se trocaram;
os fementidos Fados já deixaram
do mundo o regimento, ou desvario.
Tem o tempo sua ordem já sabida.
O mundo, não; mas anda tão confuso
que parece que dele Deus se esquece.
Casos, opiniões, natura e uso
fazem que nos pareça desta vida
que não há nela mais que o que parece.

## Confusion

When the turgid waters of the river flow by, they bring
the muddied runoff from the mountains; nearby
the once-flowering fields are parched and dry,
and the valley is cold and unproductive. The spring
and the heats of summer are gone. The transition
of things into other things continues. But it seems
as though the Fates have abandoned their usual schemes,
forsaking this world to its mostly disordered condition.
Time, of course, has order, and it never breaks
its rules, but not this world, whose chaotic strife
seems almost forgotten by God. The uncertainty
of customs, events, opinions, and nature makes
it always seem as though this life
is nothing more than what it seems to be.

---

Todas as almas tristes se mostravam
pela piadade do Feitor divino,
onde, ante o seu aspecto benino,
o devido tributo lhe pagavam.
Meus sentidos então livres estavam
(que até i foi costume o seu destino),
quando uns olhos, de que eu não era dino,
a furto de Razão me salteavam.
A nova vista me cegou de todo;
nasceu do descostume a estranheza
da suave e angélica presença.
Pera remediar-me não há i modo?
Oh! porque fez a humana natureza
entre os nascidos tanta diferença?

## Good Friday

All souls, at Mass, knelt in supplication,
in the presence of the Lord, that holy day,
within the mercy of God, to silently pray
their worship to the King of all creation.
Till then, my heart was free from every care,
and calm, according to destiny's design;
but then, those eyes, far more noble than mine,
stole my reason and left me shaken and unaware.
Her vision struck me blind with disbelief,
being such a strange and exalted state:
this new angelic presence in my heart.
Is there no way that I can find relief?
And why, at birth, does human nature create
us all so different, and so far apart?

---

Presença bela, angélica figura,
em quem, quanto o Céu tinha, nos tem dado;
gesto alegre, de rosas semeado,
entre as quais se está rindo a Fermosura;
olhos, onde tem feito tal mistura
em cristal branco e preto marchetado,
que vemos já no verde delicado
não esperança, mas enveja escura;
brandura, aviso e graça que, aumentando
a natural beleza c'um desprezo
com que, mais desprezada, mais se aumenta;
são as prisões de um coração que, preso,
seu mal ao som dos ferros vai cantando,
como faz a sereia na tormenta.

## Green Eyes

Beautiful presence, angelic figure, you've
received from heaven your special loveliness,
your perfect complexion, flush with roses, and, yes,
even Beauty smiles and stops to approve.
Your eyes are a fantastic mix of jewels,
of inlaid blacks, and crystal whites,
and that exquisite iridian green (which ignites
not hope, but the blackest envy in the pools
of your soul). Your thoughtful grace intensifies
your natural beauty, and despite the lingering pains
of his rejection, you're greatly enhanced by his disdain.
But your heart remains imprisoned, as your lovely eyes
sing out, so eerily, to the rattle of your chains,
like sirens in a raging hurricane.

---

«Quem jaz no grão sepulcro, que descreve
tão ilustres sinais no forte escudo?»
«Ninguém; que nisso, enfim, se torna tudo;
mas foi quem tudo pôde e tudo teve».
«Foi Rei?» «Fez tudo quanto a Rei se deve;
pôs na guerra e na paz devido estudo;
mas quão pesado foi ao Mouro rudo
tanto lhe seja agora a terra leve».
«Alexandre será?» «Ninguém se engane;
que sustentar mais que adquirir se estima».
«Será Adriano, grão senhor do mundo?»
«Mais observante foi da Lei de cima».
«É Numa?» «Numa, não; mas é Joane
de Portugal terceiro, sem segundo».

# Sepulcher

Who lies in this great sepulcher? Who
reclines at rest beneath this glorious shield?
No one. All things decay, and all things yield,
but once, he achieved all that a man could do.
Was he a king? He did what a king does best;
he studied the arts of justice, peace, and wars,
and soundly vanquished the encroaching Moors:
May the Earth now lightly dust his final rest.
So is it Alexander? No, no such thing:
he strove to nourish, not to subjugate.
Is it Hadrian, once "King of Everyone"?
No, he chose God's laws, not the depths of hate.
Then is it Numa? No, it's a Portuguese king:
John the Third, and second to none.

---

Ó gloriosa cruz, ó vitorioso
troféu, de despojos rodeado,
ó sinal escolhido e ordenado
para remédio tão maravilhoso;
ó fonte viva de licor sagrado,
em ti nosso mal todo foi curado!
Em ti o Senhor, que forte era chamado,
quis merecer o nome de piedoso.
Em ti se acabou o tempo da vingança;
em ti misericórdia assim floreça
como despois do inverno a primavera.
Todo o imigo ante ti desapareça.
Tu pudeste fazer tanta mudança
em quem nunca deixou de ser quem era.

## O Glorious Cross

O glorious cross, O victorious
and holy prize that encompasses everything;
O chosen miraculous sign ordained to bring
your remedy to each and every one of us.
O living font of sacred blood, expel
our sins and cure our sinful souls. In You,
O Lord, we know the almighty God, who
embodies the gentle name of mercy as well.
With You, the time of vengeance ends. A new
compassion flowers forth, forever and ever,
like after winter, when springtime blossoms again.
So vanquish all your enemies, Lord, You
who've made so many changes, yet never
cease to be exactly what You've always been.

---

Um mover d'olhos, brando e piadoso,
sem ver de qué; um riso brando e honesto,
quase forçado; um doce e humilde gesto,
de qualquer alegria duvidoso;
um despejo quieto e vergonhoso;
um repouso gravíssimo e modesto;
ũa pura bondade, manifesto
indício da alma, limpo e gracioso;
um encolhido ousar; ũa brandura;
um medo sem ter culpa; um ar sereno;
um longo e obediente sofrimento:
esta foi a celeste fermosura
da minha Circe, e o mágico veneno
que pôde transformar meu pensamento.

# Magic

The movement of her eyes, the subtle tenderness;
her quiet, honest smile, with just a trace
of reluctance; the sweet expression on her face,
somehow wary of finding happiness;
her cautious sincerity; her efficacious
ease, modest and profound; her pure
and open goodness, deeply secure
within her soul, bright and gracious.
Her thoughtful daring; her softness; her tragic
fears without guilt; her serenity, informed
by long compliant suffering. Yes, it's true,
*this* is the celestial beauty and magic
of my Circe, the venom that's transformed
everything I think, and everything I do.

---

Na metade do Céu subido ardia
o claro, almo Pastor, quando deixavam
o verde pasto as cabras, e buscavam
a frescura suave da água fria.
Co a folha da árvore sombria,
do raio ardente as aves se emparavam;
o módulo cantar, de que cessavam,
só nas roucas cigarras se sentia;
quando Liso pastor, num campo verde
Natércia, crua Ninfa, só buscava
com mil suspiros tristes que derrama.
«Porque te vás, de quem por ti se perde,
para quem pouco te ama?» suspirava.
O Eco lhe responde: «*Pouco te ama*».

## Natércia

The flaming sun rises high, to the peak
of its ascent in the sky. The goat herds shrink
away from their sweltering fields to drink
the cool refreshing waters from the creek.
The birds, burning in the scorching glare,
find shelter beneath the leaves, within the shade,
and, yet, their lovely songs begin to fade,
and only the humming cicadas fill the air.
Liso is searching for his nymph, although
he always fails, no matter how he tries,
and with a thousand sighs, bemoans his lot.
"Why have you left the one who loves you so,
for one who loves you not?" young Liso cries,
and Echo echoes softly, " . . . loves you not."

---

No mundo, poucos anos e cansados
vivi, cheios de vil miséria dura;
foi-me tão cedo a luz do dia escura
que não vi cinco lustros acabados.
Corri terras e mares apartados,
buscando à vida algum remédio ou cura;
mas aquilo que, enfim, não quer ventura,
não o alcançam trabalhos arriscados.
Criou-me Portugal na verde e cara
pátria minha Alenquer; mas ar corruto,
que neste meu terreno vaso tinha,
me fez manjar de peixes em ti, bruto
mar, que bates na Abássia fera e avara,
tão longe da ditosa pátria minha!

## Pero Moniz

In this world I managed to survive
a few short years, full of misery,
before the lights of day were taken from me,
much too soon, by the age of twenty-five.
Across vast seas in distant lands, I tried
to find some remedy for life. But when
the Fates say no, despite your efforts, again
and again, you end up defeated and unsatisfied.
Raised in Portugal, in the fertile lands
of Alenquer, I die a refugee,
dead from the foreign air and its foul decay,
food for the hungry fish in a brutish sea,
that crashes against these wild Abyssinian sands,
so unlike Alenquer, and so far away.

---

Aquela triste leda madrugada,
cheia toda de mágoa e de piedade,
enquanto houver no mundo saüdade
quero que seja sempre celebrada.
Ela só, quando amena e marchetada
saía, dando ao mundo claridade,
viu apartar-se de ũa outra vontade,
que nunca poderá ver-se apartada.
Ela só viu as lágrimas em fio
que, de uns e de outros olhos derivadas,
se acrescentaram em grande e largo rio.
Ela viu as palavras magoadas
que puderam tornar o fogo frio,
e dar descanso às almas condenadas.

## Dawn

The dawn rises lovely but ill-fated
and full of grief. For as long as heartbreaks prey
upon our tragic world, this dawning day
should be forever famous and celebrated.
Only this dawn, as her lovely lights smother
the dark, will actually see, down by the sea,
that separation that no lover can bear to see:
the parting of one love from another.
Only this dawn will see, rising above
the world, our tears flowing with burning desire,
mingling together in a river of farewell.
Only this dawn will hear these sad words of love
which will chill even the unquenchable fire
and bring relief to all the damned in hell.

---

Mudam-se os tempos, mudam-se as vontades,
muda-se o ser, muda-se a confiança;
todo o mundo é composto de mudança,
tomando sempre novas qualidades.
Continuamente vemos novidades,
diferentes em tudo da esperança;
do mal ficam as mágoas na lembrança,
e do bem—se algum houve—, as saüdades.
O tempo cobre o chão de verde manto,
que já coberto foi de neve fria,
e enfim converte em choro o doce canto.
E, afora este mudar-se cada dia,
outra mudança faz de mór espanto:
que não se muda já como soía.

## Time

Time changes, and our desires change. What we
believe—even what we are—is ever-
changing. The world *is* change, which forever
takes on new qualities. And constantly,
we see the new and the novel overturning
the past, unexpectedly, while we retain
from evil, nothing but its terrible pain,
from good (if there's been any), only the yearning.
Time covers the ground with her cloak of green
where, once, there was freezing snow—and rearranges
my sweetest songs to sad laments. Yet even more
astonishing is yet another unseen
change within all these endless changes:
that for me, *nothing* ever changes anymore.

---

Cá nesta Babilónia, donde mana
matéria a quanto mal o mundo cria;
cá onde o puro Amor não tem valia,
que a Mãe, que manda mais, tudo profana;
cá, onde o mal se afina e o bem se dana,
e pode mais que a honra a tirania;
cá, onde a errada e cega Monarquia
cuida que um nome vão a desengana;
cá, neste labirinto, onde a nobreza
com esforço e saber pedindo vão
às portas da cobiça e da vileza;
cá neste escuro caos de confusão,
cumprindo o curso estou da natureza.
Vê se me esquecerei de ti, Sião!

## Exile

Here in this Babylon, that's festering
forth as much evil as the rest of the earth;
Here where true Love deprecates his worth,
as his powerful mother pollutes everything.
Here where evil is refined and good is cursed,
and tyranny, not honor, has its way;
Here where the Monarchy, in disarray,
blindly attempts to mislead God, and worse.
Here in this labyrinth, where Royalty,
willingly, chooses to succumb
before the Gates of Greed and Infamy;
Here in this murky chaos and delirium,
I carry out my tragic destiny,
but never will I forget you, Jerusalem!

*Alegra-te, ó guerreira Lusitânia . . .*

---

Debaixo desta pedra está metido,
das sanguinosas armas descansado,
o capitão ilustre, assinalado,
Dom Fernando de Casto esclarecido.
Por todo o Oriente tão temido,
e da enveja da fama tão cantado,
este, pois, só agora sepultado,
está aqui já em terra convertido.
Alegra-te, ó guerreira Lusitânia,
por este Viriato que criaste;
e chora-o, perdido, eternamente.
Exemplo toma nisto de Dardânia;
que, se a Roma co ele aniquilaste,
nem por isso Cartago está contente.

# Dom Fernando

Beneath this stone, far from all the harms
and bloody weapons of war, there lies in peace,
Dom Fernando de Castro, the Portuguese
Captain and illustrious man-at-arms.
Once so feared in the Eastern hemisphere
that even the envious sang his praise, and now
so recently buried in the ground and somehow
transforming himself to dust, he lies right here.
But rejoice, warlike Portugal, for you
have spawned, like Viriathus, another elite,
immortal hero. Lament his loss, but remind
yourselves of the resilient Romans who knew
that even their destruction and defeat
never gave Carthage any peace of mind.

---

Doces águas e claras do Mondego,
doce repouso de minha lembrança,
onde a comprida e pérfida esperança
longo tempo após si me trouxe cego:
de vós me aparto; mas, porém, não nego
que inda a memória longa, que me alcança,
me não deixa de vós fazer mudança;
mas quanto mais me alongo, mais me achego.
Bem pudera Fortuna este instrumento
d' alma levar por terra nova e estranha,
oferecido ao mar remoto e vento;
mas alma, que de cá vos acompanha,
nas asas do ligeiro pensamento,
para vós, águas, voa, e em vós se banha.

## Mondego

Sweet, clear waters of the Mondego, sweet, kind,
and restful river of my memories,
where once misleading hopes whirled in the breeze,
misguiding me, and leaving me blind.
And now, I've gone away, sweet distant stream,
but, still, your memory overtakes me yet,
and never lets me change, or ever forget:
that the further away I am, the closer I seem.
Yes, the Fates have caused my soul to disappear
into remote and distant lands, to roam
within these seas and winds, both strange and new,
and yet, my soul, thinking of you, even here,
flies upon the wings of my sweet dreams of home
into your lovely waters and bathes in you.

---

Que modo tão sutil da Natureza,
para fugir ao mundo e seus enganos,
permite que se esconda, em tenros anos,
debaixo de um burel tanta beleza!
Mas esconder-se não pode aquela alteza
e gravidade de olhos soberanos,
a cujo resplandor entre os humanos
resistência não sinto, ou fortaleza.
Quem quer livre ficar de dor e pena,
vento-a ou trazendo-a na memória,
na mesma razão sua se condena.
Porque quem mereceu ver tanta glória,
cativo há-de ficar; que Amor ordena
que de juro tenha ela esta vitória.

## Escape

How strange is life that she should choose to shun
the world, to run away from its deceit,
to hide her youth and beauty, and to retreat
beneath the cloak of a Franciscan nun!
But nothing can conceal her grace, mystique,
and marvelous eyes, nothing on earth can hide
her beauty which leaves me totally mystified,
without resistance, helpless and weak.
Whoever keeps her image in mind,
will never be free from pain and all these misguided
hopes and desires which Reason condemns. Whoever,
like me, has seen this glorious woman will find
himself enslaved, for Love has already decided
that she has conquered my heart forever.

---

«Que levas, cruel Morte?» «Um claro dia».
«A que horas o tomaste?» «Amanhecendo».
«Entendes o que levas?» «Não o entendo».
«Pois quem to faz levar?» «Quem o entendia».
«Seu corpo quem o goza?» «A terra fria».
«Como ficou sua luz?» «Anoitecendo».
«Lusitânia que diz?» «Fica dizendo:
Enfim, não mereci Dona Maria».
«Mataste quem a viu?» «Já morto estava».
«Que diz o cru Amor?» «Falar não ousa».
«E quem o faz calar?» «Minha vontade».
«Na corte que ficou?» «Saudade brava».
«Que fica lá que ver?» «Nenhũa cousa;
mas fica que chorar sua beldade».

## Dona Maria

ON HER DEATH IN 1578

"Death, what have you stolen?"—"This lovely day."
"When did you do it?"—"At the rising sun."
"Do you have any idea whom you've taken?"—"None."
"Who willed it?"—"God, in His inscrutable way."
"Where's the corpse?"—"In the earth, in the cold."
"What's become of her brightness?"—"Dark and black."
"What says Portugal?"—"She wants her back:
convinced that Maria deserved to live and grow old."
"Did you kill those with her?"—"They're already dead."
"So what says Love?"—"She can't say a thing."
"Well, why's she so silent?"—"I've made her acquiesce."
"So what's remains at the royal court?"—"Just dread."
"What else?"—"Nothing. Not a single thing,
except lamenting her vanished loveliness."

---

Senhor João Lopes, o meu baixo estado
ontem vi posto em grau tão excelente
que vós, que sois enveja a toda a gente,
só por mim vos quiséreis ver trocado.
Vi o gesto suave e delicado
que já vos fez, contente e descontente,
lançar ao vento a voz tão docemente
que fez o ar sereno e sossegado.
Vi-lhe em poucas palavras dizer quanto
ninguém diria em muitas; eu só, cego,
magoado fiquei na doce fala.
Mas mal haja a Fortuna e o Moça cego:
um, porque os corações obriga a tanto;
outra, porque os estados desiguala.

## Senhor João Lopes

Senhor Lopes: yesterday my poor
and lowly position was briefly undone,
and even you, admired by everyone,
would have traded places with me, I'm sure.
I was privileged to see the charming face
that, once, made you content, yet discontent.
She voiced her thoughts to the wind. She lent
to the world her calm and tender grace.
She was so lovely, saying so much in just one
or two words. Her voice was like a wounding delight
that left me in a love-struck, blinded condition.
So damned be Cupid and the Fates: the Son
of Venus for binding my heart; the Sisters of Night
for entrapping me in this hopeless social position.

---

Orfeu enamorado que tañía
por la perdida ninfa, que buscaba,
en el Orco implacable donde estaba,
con la arpa y con la voz la enternecía.
La rueda de Ixión no se movia,
ningún atormentado se quejaba,
las penas de los otros ablandaba,
y todas las de todos él sentía.
El son pudo obligar de tal manera,
que, en dulce galardón de lo cantado,
los infernales reyes, condolidos,
le mandaron volver su compañera,
y volvióla á perder el desdichado,
con que fueron entrambos los perdidos.
{Spanish}

# Orpheus

Orpheus gently sings his love-sick passion
for Eurydice, his wife, who's trapped in hell,
and with his harp and voice, he weaves a spell
that conjures up such pity and compassion
that the Wheel of Ixion stops. So long
as Orpheus continues to sing, the tortured souls
in hell forget their pain—since he consoles
them all, sensing their pain, with his lovely song.
His music is so affecting and serene
that he's rewarded in that dreadful place
by the infernal kings of hell, who then
command his wife's return to earth, unseen—
but Orpheus turns, impatient to see her face,
and, desperately, they lose each other again.

---

Sempre, cruel Senhora, receei,
medindo vossa grã desconfiança,
que desse em desamor vossa tardança,
e que me perdesse eu, pois vos amei.
Perca-se, enfim, já tudo o que esperei,
pois noutro amor já tendes esperança.
Tão patente será vossa mudança
quanto eu encobri sempre o que vos dei.
Dei-vos a alma, a vida e o sentido;
de tudo o que em mim há vos fiz senhora.
Prometeis e negais o mesmo Amor.
Agora tal estou que, de perdido,
não sei por onde vou; mas algũ' hora
vos dará tal lembrança grande dor.

## Cruel Senhora

Cruel Senhora, I've always been wary. I knew
I needed to watch you closely in case
your doubts would surge to disaffection and erase
our love. Then I'd be ruined, since I love only you.
And now, everything I'd hope to have is lost:
you're pursuing another lover. So I detach
myself, believing your retribution will match
the sacrificial depths my love has cost:
I've given my soul, my senses, and my life to you;
I've given you everything I have within me,
and you promised love, but now, there's only disdain.
Lost and hopeless, I don't know what to do,
yet I know the day will come when this memory
will crush you down with terrifying pain.

---

Tornai essa brancura à alva açucena,
e essa purpúrea cor às puras rosas;
tornai ao sol as chamas luminosas
dessa vista que a roubos vos condena.
Tornai à suavíssima sirena
dessa voz as cadências deleitosas;
tornai a graça às Graças, que queixosas
estão de a ter por vós menos serena.
Tornai à bela Vénus a beleza;
a Minerva o saber, o engenho e a arte;
e a pureza à castíssima Diana.
Despojai-vos de toda essa grandeza
de dões; e ficareis em toda a arte
convosco só, que é só ser inumana.

## Essence

Give back your whiteness to the Easter flowers,
and your blushes to the crimson rose;
Give back to the sun the luminous light that glows
from your ravishing eyes and overpowers
our hearts. Give back your songs to the Sirens, who
filled your voice with irresistible harmony;
Give back your charms to the Graces, who now agree
they're much less elegant than you.
Give back to beautiful Venus your loveliness,
to Minerva your wisdom, talents, and refined
arts, and give back your purity to the chaste and true
Diana. Divest yourself of all you now possess,
all these gifts, and all that's left behind
is cruelty . . . the very essence of you.

---

O cisne, quando sente ser chegada
a hora que põe termo a sua vida,
música com voz alta e mui subida
levanta pola praia inhabitada.
Deseja ter a vida prolongada,
chorando do viver a despedida:
com grande saüdade da partida,
celebra o triste fim desta jornada.
Assi, Senhora minha, quando via
o triste fim que davam meus amores,
estando posto já no extremo fio,
com mais suave canto e harmonia
descantei, pelos vossos desfavores,
*la vuestra falsa fe, y el amor mío.*

## Swan

The swan, when it senses that little more
of life remains, that its time has come to die,
sings out a song, a subtle lovely cry,
beside the sea, along the lonely shore.
It longs for more, it wishes to extend
its life, but can't, and so it wails its last
farewell in song, mourning what's lost and past,
celebrating its journey's bitter end.
And now, my lady, since I can also see
the imminent sad end of my life and love,
which hangs by a thread that's stretched and frayed,
I sing an even sweeter melody—
of your disregard, of falsity, of
unfaithfulness, of all my love betrayed.

---

Os reinos e os impérios poderosos,
que em grandeza no mundo mais creceram,
ou por valor de esforço floreceram
ou por varões nas letras espantosos.
Teve Grécia Temístocles famosos;
os Cipiões a Roma engrandeceram;
doze pares a França glória deram;
Cides a Espanha, e Laras belicosos.
Ao nosso Portugal (que agora vemos
tão diferente de seu ser primeiro),
os vossos deram honra e liberdade.
E em vós, grão sucessor e novo herdeiro
do bragançāo estado, há mil extremos
iguais ao sangue, e móres que a idade.

## Dom Teodósio

Every kingdom and powerful empire that's been
renowned in the world owns its pre-eminence
to certain valorous leaders of excellence,
or to the arts of its literary men.
Greece blossomed under famed Themistocles' reign;
the Scipios guided Rome's great advance;
the dozen Peers immortalized young France,
as did the Cids and the Seven Laras in Spain.
And Portugal (now falling into disrepair)
was given its freedom and honor by your wise
and bold ancestors, the Braganza cavaliers.
And now, in you, their worthy successor and heir,
a thousand, noble, magnificent virtues arise
in your blood—unequalled by anyone so young in years.

---

Ilustre e dino ramo dos Meneses,
aos quais o prudente e largo Céu
(que errar não sabe), em dote concedeu
rompesse os maométicos arneses;
desprezando a Fortuna e seus revezes,
ide para onde o Fado vos moveu;
erguei flamas no mar alto Eritreu,
e sereis nova luz aos Portugueses.
Oprimi com tão firme e forte peito
o Pirata insolente, que se espante
e trema Taprobana e Gedrosia.
Dai nova causa à cor do árabo estreito:
assi que o roxo mar, daqui em diante,
o seja só co sangue de Turquia.

## Dom Fernando de Meneses

Illustrious and worthy scion, flower
of the Meneses line, the generous heavens ordain
you special gifts and talents for your campaign
to crush the Islamic mass and Muslim power.
Go forth wherever Fate might lead, and seize
the day, scoffing at Fortune's foolish games,
then light up the Eritrean Sea in flames,
and become a brilliant light to the Portuguese.
With fearlessness and courage, follow the Fates,
smash the pirates, frighten Ceylon, bring dread
to awed Gedrosia, and as you work
your destiny, recolor the Arabian Straits:
make the so-called Red Sea truly red,
brightly dyed with the blood of the hated Turk.

---

Erros meus, má fortuna, amor ardente
em minha perdição se conjuraram;
os erros e a fortuna sobejaram,
que para mim bastava o amor somente.
Tudo passei; mas tenho tão presente
a grande dor das cousas, que passaram,
que as magoadas iras me ensinaram
a não querer já nunca ser contente.
Errei todo o discurso de meus anos;
dei causa que a Fortuna castigasse
as minhas mal fundadas esperanças.
De amor não vi senão breves enganos.
Oh! quem tanto pudesse que fartasse
este meu duro génio de vinganças!

## Doom

My sins, my wild loves, and Fate herself
have all conspired against me. My countless tough-
breaks and dumb mistakes have been hard enough,
especially, since all I ever wanted was love itself.
Somehow, I've survived, yet I still possess
the terrible pains of everything that's passed—
as all those whirling Furies convinced me, at last,
to never, ever hope for happiness.
Over the years of my life, I still can recall
those endless mistakes and blunders that incited Fate
to punish my foolish hopes so relentlessly.
Unfortunately, deceitful love offered no help at all.
Oh, what could ever possibly satiate
this evil spirit of vengeance that's torturing me!

---

Lindo e sutil trançado, que ficaste
em penhor do remédio que mereço,
se só contigo, vendo-te, endoudeço,
que fora cos cabelos que apertaste?
Aquelas tranças de ouro que ligaste,
que os raios do Sol têm em pouco preço,
não sei se para engano do que peço,
se para me atar, os desataste.
Lindo trançado, em minhas mãos te vejo,
e por satisfação de minhas dores
(como quem não tem outra) hei-de tomar-te.
E se não for contente meu desejo,
dir-lhe ei que, nesta regra dos amores,
pelo todo também se toma a parte.

## Ribbon

Beautiful, so subtle ribbon, you
are the substitute for her love. She's left you behind,
and seeing you drives me out of my mind!
(Imagine what seeing her lovely hair would do?)
You, who held those golden braids above
her face—her hair glowing like the sun's gold fire:
Have you been left to mock my useless desire?
Or to bind me further to my foolish love?
Beautiful ribbon, I'll keep you to provide
some recompense for my painful loss and shame
(like one who's got nothing left, just his broken heart).
And if my love will never be satisfied,
I'll still admit to you that, in this game
of love: for the sake of the whole, I'll keep this part.

---

Num bosque que das Ninfas se habitava,
Sílvia, Ninfa linda, andava um dia;
subida nũa árvore sombria,
as amarelas flores apanhava.
Cupido, que ali sempre costumava
a vir passar a sesta à sombra fria,
num ramo o arco e setas que trazia,
antes que adormecesse, pendurava.
A Ninfa, como idóneo tempo vira
para tamanha empresa, não dilata,
mas com as armas foge ao Moço esquivo.
As setas traz nos olhos, com que tira.
Ó pastores! fugi, que a todos mata,
senão a mim, que de matar-me vivo.

# Sybil

In the woods, where the nymphs pass their hours,
Sybil, the loveliest nymph, decides one day
to climb a shady tree, making her way
into the branches to pluck its yellow flowers.
Then Cupid, planning his usual siesta, deep
within the lovely shaded woods, comes by
and hangs his famous bow and arrow high
within those branches before he falls to sleep.
So Sybil, seizing the opportunity, spies
the weapons of the sleeping god, then flees
with his bow and arrow, racing in a blaze
of speed, carrying the love-darts in her eyes.
So shepherds, run! She kills everyone she sees!
Except me—who lives for nothing but her deadly gaze.

---

Dizei, Senhora, da Beleza ideia:
para fazerdes esse áureo crino,
onde fostes buscar esse ouro fino?
De que escondida mina ou de que veia?
Dos vossos olhos essa luz febeia,
esse respeito, de um império dino?
Se o alcançastes com saber divino,
se com encantamentos de Medeia?
De que escondidas conchas escolhestes
as perlas preciosas orientais
que, falando, mostrais no doce riso?
Pois vos formastes tal como quisestes,
vigiai-vos de vós, não vos vejais;
fugi das fontes: lembre-vos Narciso.

## Perfection

You're the perfect beauty. So please explain,
my Love, your lovely, golden, flowing hair?
Where could you find a gold so brilliant and rare?
Within some secret mine or hidden vein?
And how did your eyes capture the solar light?
Did you seize Apollo's flaming majesty
with sacred wisdom and godlike subtlety?
Or with Medean enchantments in the night?
From which hidden shells did you choose those rare
and precious Oriental pearls that grace
your smile whenever you laugh? But wait,
since you're perfectly formed, my Love, beware:
shun all fountains, never look at your face,
remember Narcissus, remember his fate.

---

Senhora já dest' alma, perdoai
de um vencido de Amor os desatinos;
e sejam vossos olhos tão beninos
com este puro amor, que d' alma sai.
A minha pura fé somente olhai,
e vede meus extremos se são finos;
e se de algũa pena forem dinos,
em mim, Senhora minha, vos vingai.
Não seja a dor, que abrasa o triste peito,
causa por onde pene o coração,
que tanto em firme amor vos é sujeito.
Guardai-vos do que alguns, Dama, dirão;
que, sendo raro em tudo vosso objeito,
possa morar em vós ingratidão.

## Punishment

Lady, mistress of my heart, console
your vanquished lover; forgive my mad
and rash mistakes, look gently on the sad
but pure, sweet love that rages within my soul.
Look and see the endless devotion of
my heart; see if my proofs of love are tender,
and if they're not, then quickly render
your penalties and punishments, my love.
But keep these pains, which destroy me every day,
from consuming my heart, which, in despair,
loves you, as always, humble and subdued.
And guard yourself, my Lady, let no one say
that within the soul of one so perfect and rare,
there might be found the sin of ingratitude.

---

Se pena por amar-vos se merece,
quem dela livre está, ou quem isento?
Que alma, que razão, qu' entendimento
em ver-vos se não rende e obedece?
Que mór glória na vida s' oferece
que ocupar-se em vós o pensamento?
Toda a pena cruel, todo o tormento
em ver-vos se não sente, mas esquece.
Mas se merece pena quem amando
contino vos está, se vos ofende,
o mundo matareis, que todo é vosso.
Em mim podeis, Senhora, ir começando,
que claro se conhece e bem se entende
amar-vos quanto devo e quanto posso.

## Destruction

If loving you brings pain and disgrace,
then who is free? Who's exempt? What dazed
poor human soul does not surrender, having gazed,
even just once, upon your lovely face?
What greater glory does life offer, my dear,
than to be obsessed with thoughts of you?
Since every torment rings false and untrue,
and quickly vanishes as soon as you appear?
If everyone who loves you must be
destroyed, then everyone must die, forever
and ever (since everything submits to you).
So, my Senhora, begin your destruction with me,
since we both know that no one else could ever
love you as much as I can—or as much as I do.

---

Enquanto Febo os montes acendia
do Céu com luminosa claridade,
por evitar do ócio a castidade,
na caça o tempo Délia dispendia.
Vénus, que então de furto descendia,
por cativar de Anquises a vontade,
vendo Diana em tanta honestidade,
quase zombando dela, lhe dizia:
«Tu vás com tuas redes na espessura
os fugitivos cervos enredando;
mas as minhas enredam o sentido».
«Milhor é—respondia a deusa pura—
nas redes leves cervos ir tomando
que tomar-te a ti nelas teu marido».

## Diana

When Phoebus flamed the mountains with his strong
and bright and brilliant lights from heaven, the great
and chaste Diana, never idle, went straight
to the deepest woods and hunted all day long.
But frivolous Venus—descending to earth to play,
to tantalize hopeless Anchises—spied
Diana hunting through the countryside,
and called to her sister goddess in a mocking way:
"You wander these woods with your snares every year,
catching nothing but little creatures, while I,
with my nets, entrap the human heart." But then,
the huntress replied: "It's better to hunt for deer,
than to have your husband catch you as you lie
within your treacherous infidelities once again."

---

Fiou-se o coração, de muito isento
de si, cuidando mal que tomaria
tão ilícito amor tal ousadia,
tal modo nunca visto de tormento.
Mas os olhos pintaram tão a tento
outros que visto têm, na fantasia,
que a razão, temerosa do que via,
fugiu, deixando o campo ao pensamento.
«Ó Hipólito casto que, de jeito,
de Fedra, tua madraste, foste amado,
que não sabia ter nenhum respeito!
Em mim vingou o Amor teu casto peito;
mas está desse agravo tão vingado,
que se arrepende já do que tem feito».

# Hippolytus

My over-confident heart grew more and more
blinded to the evil it was capable of:
such a daring and illicit love,
such an agony never felt before.
But her eyes were like the ones that, every day,
I conjured in my foolish fantasy,
and Reason, terrified, abandoned me
to all my tempting thoughts and ran away.
O chaste Hippolytus, you took no part
in Phaedra's incestuous schemes. You never consented
to a love that blasphemed what should and shouldn't be.
So Love revenged, on me, your virtuous heart,
and now, at last, she's finally repented
for all the brutal damage she's heaped on me.

Esforço grande, igual ao pensamento;
pensamentos em obras divulgados,
e não em peito tímido encerrados
e desfeitos despois em chuva e vento;
ânimo da cobiça baixa isento,
dino por isso só de altos estados,
fero açoute dos nunca bem domados
povos do Malabar sanguinolento;
gentileza de membros corporais,
ornados de pudica continência,
obra por certo rara de natura:
estas virtudes e outras muitas mais,
dinas todas da homérica eloquência,
jazem debaixo desta sepultura.

## Epitaph

FOR DOM HENRIQUE DE MENESES

His formidable strength of will conforms
to his noble intellect; his ideals confirm
themselves in action, always bold and firm
even in life's tumultuous winds and storms:
unmoved by greed or vulgar riches; the most
remarkable exemplar of the truly
dignified state; and the scourge of all those unruly,
bloodthirsty peoples on the Malabar Coast.
Handsome in form and face, and pure before
the entire world, and chaste; an excellence
of noble attributes which seldom occur
in nature. All these virtues and many more,
worthy of Homer's highest eloquence,
are laid to rest beneath this sepulcher.

---

Se os capitães antigos colocados
naqueles triunfos altos de vitória
feriram nas orelhas vossa história,
de vergonha e temor foram pasmados.
Por terra logo todos derribados
troféus, fama e sua grão memória,
dando lugar ao louvor vosso e glória,
que sós no mundo fossem celebrados.
Na Antiguidade levam-vos vantagem
que está de errores cheia em toda parte,
como se mostra bem no que temos visto.
Vós, nas obras, feitos e linhagem
que na milícia sois o mesmo Marte
e em virtudes cumpris a lei de Cristo.

## Conquistadors

FOR DOM CONSTANTINO

Allowing the ancient captains to surpass
all others in the ranks of victory
and fame deeply wounds the truth of history,
since even they're amazed at what's come to pass.
Their fame, glory, and trophies of war
need to be diminished and abrogated,
so their place can now be given to the celebrated
and noble Portuguese conquistador.
In error-prone antiquity, the captains were all
overpraised, but now we know more than before,
aware of what others have done and sacrificed.
You, Portuguese, in your deeds and overall
accomplishments, are the equal of Mars in battle, yet more
important, in virtue, you submit to the laws of Christ.

---

Tu que descanso buscas com cuidado
neste mar do mundo tempestuoso
não esperes de achar nenhum repouso
senão em Cristo Jesus Crucificado.
Se por riquezas vives desvelado,
em Deus está o tesouro mais precioso;
se estás de fermosura desejoso,
se olhas este Senhor ficas namorado.
Se tu buscas deleites ou prazeres,
nele está o dulçor dos dulçores
que a todos nos deleita com vitória.
Se porventura glória ou honra queres,
que maior honra poda ser nem glória
que servir ao Senhor grande dos senhores?

## Refuge

You who seek serenity in the wide
tempestuous sea of the world, cease
and abandon all hope of ever finding peace,
except in Jesus Christ, God Crucified.
If wealth absorbs your thoughts and preoccupies
your nights, God is the greatest treasure of all;
And if you're looking for beauty, always recall
that God alone is the Beauty that satisfies.
If you seek delights to set your heart on fire,
remember that God's the sweetest of all, Who rewards
His followers with victory at last;
If honor and glory are what you most desire,
no greater honor or glory has ever surpassed
humbly serving the highest Lord of Lords.

---

Verdade, Amor, Razão, Merecimento
qualquer alma farão segura e forte;
porém, Fortuna, Caso, Tempo e Sorte
têm do confuso mundo o regimento.
Efeitos mil revolve o pensamento
e não sabe a que causa se reporte;
mas sabe que o que é mais que vida e morte,
que não o alcança humano entendimento.
Doctos varões darão razões subidas;
mas são experiências mais provadas,
e por isso é milhor ter muito visto.
Cousas há i que passam sem ser cridas
e cousas cridas há sem ser passadas . . .
Mas o milhor de tudo é crer em Cristo.

## Belief

Truth, Love, Reason, and Merit can touch
every soul and make it firm and strong,
but Time, Luck, Chance, and Fate have long
ruled over this world that troubles us so much.
Our thoughts contain a thousand things, yet we're resigned
to never know their cause. And though we crave
to know what lies beyond this life and the grave,
we know it's inaccessible to the human mind.
Lofty speculations have been conceived
by philosophers, yet experience is always preferred,
since seeing always seems better and more precise.
Yet so many things that *have* happened are not believed,
and so many things are believed that *never* occurred . . .
So the best of all is to believe in Jesus Christ.

*«Porque a tamanhas penas se oferece,*
*pelo pecado alheio e erro insano,*
*o trino Deus?» . . .*

---

«Porque a tamanhas penas se oferece,
pelo pecado alheio e erro insano,
o trino Deus?»—«Porque o sujeito humano
não pode co castigo que merece».
«Quem padecerá as penas que padece?
Quem sofrerá desonra, morte e dano?»
«Ninguém, senão se for o soberano
que reina, e servos manda, e obedece».
Foi a força do homem tão pequena
que não pôde suster tanta aspereza,
pois não susteve a lei que Deus ordena.
Sofre-a aquela imensa Fortaleza,
por puro amor; que a humanal fraqueza
foi para o erro, e não já para a pena.

## The Passion

So why has the triune God, in agony,
sacrificed Himself for the insane sin
of Man? Because no man could ever begin
to withstand the just and heavy penalty.
Who could endure the necessary pains?
Who could suffer such injury, death, and disgrace?
No one, except for God, whose sovereign grace
commands, and reigns, and obeys, as He ordains.
The resources of men are way too weak and small;
they could never sustain the pain of God's just plan
for righteous and necessary restitution.
So God's great strength endures it all,
with a pure and merciful love for helpless Man:
who makes the error, but never the retribution.

---

Alma minha gentil, que te partiste
tão cedo desta vida descontente,
repousa lá no Céu eternamente,
e viva eu cá na terra sempre triste.
Se lá no assento etéreo, onde subiste,
memória desta vida se consente,
não te esqueças daquele amor ardente
que já nos olhos meus tão puro viste.
E se vires que pode merecer-te
algũa cousa a dor que me ficou
da mágoa, sem remédio, de perder-te,
roga a Deus, que teus anos encurtou,
que tão cedo de cá me leve a ver-te,
quão cedo de meus olhos te levou.

## Dear Gentle Soul

Dear gentle soul, who has, too soon, departed
this life, so discontent: please rest, my dear,
forever in heaven, while I, remaining here,
must live alone, in pain, and brokenhearted.
Within your ethereal state, so high above,
if you are allowed to recall your life below,
remember what you saw, not long ago,
within my eyes, my perfect ardent love.
And if my pain has earned me some relief,
some dispensation, I wonder if you might
in prayer, ask God, who took away your brief
young life, if He would soon, this very night,
give me death, and end my helpless grief,
as swiftly as He took you from my sight.

---

Eu cantarei de amor tão docemente,
por uns termos em si tão concertados
que dous mil acidentes namorados
faça sentir ao peito que não sente.
Farei que amor a todos avivente,
pintando mil segredos delicados,
brandas iras, suspiros magoados,
temerosa ousadia e pena ausente.
Também, Senhora, do desprezo honesto
de vossa vista branda e rigorosa
contentar-me-ei dizendo a menos parte.
Porém, para cantar de vosso gesto
a composição alta e milagrosa,
aqui falta saber, engenho e arte.

## Song of Love

I'll sing a song of love so sweet, so blessed
with harmonious sounds, so true to the name
of love (with two thousand examples), it will enflame
even those with dead hearts in their chest.
My song will ignite new love in everyone,
painting the thousand mysteries: the caring
angers, the beautiful sighs, the dreadful daring,
and all the pains of love that's come undone.
And yet, I'll say so very little, my Love,
about your rigorous virtue—about the true
but scrupulous look in your lovely eyes. Sweetheart,
I won't attempt to sing of you, or of
the miraculous, lofty essence of you,
because I lack the skill, the genius, and the art.

---

Árvore, cujo pomo, belo e brando,
natureza de leite e sangue pinta,
onde a pureza, de vergonha tinta,
está virgíneas faces imitando;
nunca da ira e do vento, que arrancando
os troncos vão, o teu injúria sinta;
nem por malícia de ar te seja extinta
a cor, que está teu fruito debuxando.
Que pois me emprestas doce e idóneo abrigo
a meu contentamento, e favoreces
com teu suave cheiro minha glória,
se não te celebrar como mereces,
cantando-te, sequer farei contigo
doce, nos casos tristes, a memória.

## Rose-Apple Tree

Lovely tree, whose beautiful and lush,
soft fruit is colored red like blood and white
like milk, and imitates the subtle light
complexion of the lovely virgin's blush.
Never will the raging winds uproot
your trunks, nor injure you. And never
will any dark or noxious vapors ever
diminish the colors of your lovely fruit.
Once, you lent your shady shelter, kind tree,
to my love, and bathed her in the gentle spell
of your sweet and fragrant scent. And so, if some
of the time, my song has failed to praise you well
enough, remember that your memory will be
my only refuge in the sorrowful times to come.

---

Está o lascivo e doce passarinho
com o biquinho as penas ordenando,
o verso sem medida, alegre e brando,
espedindo no rústico raminho.
O cruel caçador (que do caminho
se vem calado e manso desviando),
na pronta vista a seta endireitando,
lhe dá no Estígio Lago eterno ninho.
Destarte o coração, que livre andava,
(posto que já de longe destinado)
onde menos temia, foi ferido.
Porque o Frecheiro cego me esperava,
para que me tomasse descuidado,
em vossos claros olhos escondido.

## Little Bird

The carefree little bird, preoccupied
with preening its lovely feathers, sings
its joyful tunes, unrestrained, and rings
its happiness throughout the countryside.
But the cruel hunter (who stealthily comes from beyond
the beaten path) stops, and, straightaway,
he aims his arrow and fires, blasting his prey
into eternal rest beside the Stygian pond.
Just like my carefree heart (which once beat free,
although it was already doomed) was shot,
so unaware, caught in a blind surprise
by sightless Cupid who aimed and fired at me,
his unsuspecting prey, from his secret spot—
hidden and camouflaged within your brilliant eyes.

*Vencido está de Amor . . .*

---

*V*encido está de Amor
*o* mais que pode ser
*s*ujeita a vos servir
*o*ferecendo tudo
*C*ontente deste bem,
*o*u hora em que se viu
*m*il vezes desejando
*o*utra vez renovar
*C*om essa pretensão
*a* causa que me guia
*t*ão estranha, tão doce,
*J*urando não seguir
*v*otando só por vós
*o*u ser no vosso amor

*m*eu pensamento
*v*encida a vida,
*i*nstituída,
*a* vosso intento.
*l*ouva o momento
*t*ão bem perdida;
*a* tal ferida
*s*eu perdimento.
*e*stá segura
*n*esta empresa,
*h*onrosa e alta.
*o*utra ventura,
*r*ara firmeza,
*a*chado em falta.

# For Caterina

<table>
<tr><td>I'm vanquished by your love.</td><td>My thoughts aspire,</td></tr>
<tr><td>always, to you, my dear, they</td><td>yield to you</td></tr>
<tr><td>my life, having only one</td><td>purpose: to</td></tr>
<tr><td>yield everything to your</td><td>every desire.</td></tr>
<tr><td>Often, I recall that first,</td><td>ecstatic, star-crossed,</td></tr>
<tr><td>unequalled moment, still</td><td>ravenous to</td></tr>
<tr><td>revive, a thousand times, my</td><td>love for you,</td></tr>
<tr><td>craving that "wounding" again,</td><td>eager to be "lost."</td></tr>
<tr><td>Always, I have just one,</td><td>single ambition:</td></tr>
<tr><td>praising you—which guides my</td><td>soul forever—</td></tr>
<tr><td>to serve your sweet, exalted</td><td>love, and pursue,</td></tr>
<tr><td>in all my days to come, no</td><td>other mission,</td></tr>
<tr><td>vowing to serve only you,</td><td>vowing to never</td></tr>
<tr><td>end up complacent, or</td><td>end up failing you.</td></tr>
</table>

---

Quando de minhas mágoas a comprida
maginação os olhos me adormece,
em sonhos aquela alma me aparece
que para mim foi sonho nesta vida.
Lá nũa soïdade, onde estendida
a vista pelo campo desfalece,
corro para ela; e ela então parece
que mais de mim se alonga, compelida.
Brado: «Não me fujais, sombra benina!»
Ela—os olhos em mim cum brando pejo,
como quem diz que já não pode ser—,
torna a fugir-me; e eu, gritando: «*Dina* . . . »
antes que diga *mene,* acordo, e vejo
que nem um breve engano posso ter.

## Dinamene

When my fantasies, and these extreme
regrets, shut my eyes in sleep, I discover,
before me, the risen spirit of my lover,
who was, even in life, always a dream.
Then across some desert, where I can barely see
the endlessly distant horizon, I pursue
my love without success. She fades from view,
by some unseen force, and glides away from me.
I cry out, "Spirit, don't run away again!"
but her eyes meet mine, sad and soft and deep,
as if to say, "No. This can never be!"
She starts to leave. I scream: "Dina . . . ," but then,
before I finish her name, I wake from sleep,
as even this brief delusion escapes from me.

---

Na ribeira do Eufrates assentado,
discorrendo me achei pela memória
aquele breve bem, aquela glória,
que em ti, doce Sião, tinha passado.
Da causa de meus males perguntado
me foi: «Como não cantas a história
de teu passado bem, e da vitória
que sempre de teu mal hás alcançado?
Não sabes que, a quem canta, se lhe esquece
o mal, inda que grave e rigoroso?
Canta, pois, e não chores dessa sorte».
Respondo com suspiros: «Quando crece
a muita saüdade, o piadoso
remédio é não cantar senão a morte».

## Euphrates

Sitting where the rapid waters flow,
on the banks of the Euphrates, I think of my past,
and all the blessings which faded away so fast
back in my youth, in Zion, years ago.
But then, a sudden voice addresses my fears
and the source of all my misfortunes: "Why not sing?
Sing how you've overcome your suffering.
Or sing about your happy early years.
Surely you know that he who sings forgets,
even his most tragic and obstinate
pain? Don't curse your present fate, just try
to sing!" But I sadly reply, "When sorrow gets
so overwhelming, the only compassionate
remedy is *not* to sing—but to die."

---

Aquela que, de pura castidade,
de si mesma tomou cruel vingança
por ũa breve e súbita mudança
contrária à sua honra e qualidade,
venceu à fermosura a honestidade,
venceu no fim da vida a esperança,
por que ficasse viva tal lembrança,
tal amor, tanta fé, tanta verdade.
De si, da gente e do mundo esquecida,
feriu com duro ferro o brando peito,
banhando em sangue a força do tirano.
Estranha ousadia! estranho feito!
Que, dando breve morte ao corpo humano,
tenha sua memória larga vida!

# Lucretia

Lucretia, inspired by her sense
of ideal chastity, terminated
her life after the rape that violated
her Roman honor and noble innocence.
Valuing virtue more than life itself,
she abandoned the hopes and dreams that she
once had, but kept alive her memory—
her love, her faith, and her truth. Forgetting herself,
and everything else, when the time was right,
she plunged into her chest with the cold steel knife
and bathed in blood the tyrant's vicious crime.
Amazing courage! Amazing death! Yet despite
that sudden end to Lucretia's earthly life,
her memory will last until the end of time.

---

Que vençais no Oriente tanto reis,
que de novo nos deis da Índia o estado,
que escureçais a fama que ganhado
tinham os que ganharam a infiéis;
que do tempo tenhais vencido as leis,
que tudo, enfim, vençais co tempo armado;
mais é vencer na pátria, desarmado,
os monstros e as quimeras que venceis.
E assi, sobre vencerdes tanto imigo,
e por armas fazer que, sem segundo,
vosso nome no mundo ouvido seja,
o que vos dá mais nome inda no mundo
é vencerdes, Senhor, no Reino amigo,
tantas ingratidões, tão grande enveja!

## Luís de Ataíde

More than crushing countless kings, those lords
of the Orient; more than preserving the state
of India; more than eclipsing the fate
and fame of others who'd fought the heathen hordes;
more—far more—than all those grand
and marvelous military campaigns, is the way
in which you now, completely unarmed, slay
the monsters and chimeras of our native land.
Over the years, accomplishing so much,
and crushing your enemies, your name is now
unparalleled in fame and majesty,
and yet, what inspires your greatest praise is how
you've vanquished, my Lord, in Portugal, such
ingratitude—such awesome jealousy!

---

Sete anos de pastor Jacob servia
Labão, pai de Raquel, serrana bela;
mas não servia ao pai, servia a ela,
e a ela só por prémio pretendia.
Os dias, na esperança de um só dia,
passava, contentando-se com vê-la;
porém o pai, usando de cautela,
em lugar de Raquel lhe dava Lia.
Vendo o triste pastor que com enganos
lhe fora assi negada a sua pastora,
como se a não tivera merecida,
começa de servir outros sete anos,
dizendo: «Mais servira, se não fora
para tão longo amor tão curta a vida».

# Jacob

For seven years, the shepherd Jacob slaved
for the father of beautiful Rachel, working not for the man,
but only for her, knowing ever since he began
that she alone was the only reward he craved.
His days, dreaming of the wedding that lay ahead,
passed by, content to see her from time to time,
until her father plotted his duplicitous crime,
by placing Leah in Jacob's marriage bed.
Learning the cruel deception, Jacob, in tears,
had lost the one he loved, as if, somehow,
he hadn't truly earned the proper wife.
But he starts all over again, for seven more years,
saying, "If life wasn't so short, beginning right now,
I serve even longer for Rachel, the love of my life."

---

Debaixo desta pedra sepultada
jaz do mundo a mais nobre fermosura,
a quem a Morte, só de inveja pura,
sem tempo sua vida tem roubada,
sem ter respeito àquela assim estremada
gentileza de luz, que a noite escura
tornava em claro dia, cuja alvura
do Sol a clara luz tinha eclipsada.
Do Sol peitada foste, cruel Morte,
pera o livrar de quem o escurecia;
e da Lũa que, ante ela, luz não tinha.
Como de tal poder tiveste sorte?
E, se a tiveste, como tão asinha
tornaste a luz do mundo em terra fria?

## Caterina

Beneath this gravestone lies the most sublime
and noble beauty in all the world, dispatched
by cruel and petty Death, who snatched
her from this earthly life before her time,
without the slightest respect for all she'd done
with her life—whose radiance transformed the night
to brightest day, whose brilliant, stunning light
even eclipsed the great and luminous sun.
But then, cruel Death, the jealous sun swore a vow
to murder the one who'd obscured his light. And the moon,
envious as well, joined the sun and gave
their bribes to you. How could you have such power? How
could you extinguished so fast, so soon,
the light of this world beneath this cold, dirt grave?

---

O céu, a terra, o vento sossegado;
as ondas, que se estendem pela areia;
os peixes, que no mar o sono enfreia;
o nocturno silêncio repousado . . .
O pescador Aónio que, deitado
onde co vento a água se meneia,
chorando, o nome amado em vão nomeia,
que não pode ser mais que nomeado.
«Ondas—dezia—, antes que Amor me mate,
tornai-me a minha Ninfa, que tão cedo
me fizestes à morte estar sujeita».
Ninguém lhe fala. O mar, de longe, bate;
move-se brandamente o arvoredo . . .
Leva-lhe o vento a voz, que ao vento deita.

# The Wind

The sky, the earth, and the wind are blessed
with calm tonight; the waves reach for the shore;
the fish are lulled to sleep; and more and more,
the silent night is full of peace and rest.
At least, until the young fisherman came—
who lying down, where the winds are whirling above
the sea, wails in vain the name of his love,
who now is nothing more, nor less, than a name.
"Waves!" he cries, "This grief is killing me! Before
I die, return my lovely nymph, whom you
have cruelly drowned to death for ever and ever."
But nothing replies. The ocean still beats the shore;
the trees still softly stir; and the residue
of his fading voice is lost on the wind forever.

---

Em prisões baixas fui um tempo atado,
vergonhoso castigo de meus erros;
inda agora arrojando levo os ferros
que a Morte, a meu pesar, tem já quebrado.
Sacrifiquei a vida a meu cuidado,
que Amor não quer cordeiros nem bezerros;
vi mágoas, vi misérias, vi desterros:
parece-me que estava assi ordenado.
Contentei-me com pouco, conhecendo
que era o contentamento vergonhoso,
só por ver que cousa era viver ledo.
Mas minha estrela, que eu já 'gora entendo,
a Morte cega e o Caso duvidoso,
me fizeram de gostos haver medo.

# Prison

Restrained in many prisons, I've had to pay,
shamefully, for all that I've done wrong;
and even now, I seem to drag along
my chains, though Fate has taken them away.
I sacrificed my life to satiate
my selfish whims, but Love was never content
with such a sacrifice, so banishment
and misery became my natural fate.
I've satisfied myself with little overall,
seeking shameless love, irresponsibly
seeking lust and satiation without measure.
But now, my fateful star has shown me all
the blindnesses of life and death, and made of me:
a man who shudders at the thought of pleasure.

---

Julga-me a gente toda por perdido
vendo-me, tão entregue a meu cuidado,
andar sempre dos homens apartado
e dos tratos humanos esquecido.
Mas eu, que tenho o mundo conhecido
e quase que sobre ele ando dobrado,
tenho por baixo, rústico, enganado,
quem não é com meu mal engrandecido.
Vão revolvendo a terra, o mar e o vento,
busque riquezas, honras a outra gente,
vencendo ferro, fogo, frio e calma;
que eu só, em humilde estado, me contento
de trazer esculpido eternamente
vosso fermoso gesto dentro n'alma.

## Recluse

The whole world judges me as lost. My days
seem wasted on unrequited love,
cut off from other people, wary of
their ordinary and often insensitive ways.
I know this world too well. I know its rules.
Twice I've traveled this world, and I believe
that those who can't comprehend why I grieve
and suffer are shallow, self-deluded fools.
O Earth, and Sea, and Wind! Others were meant
to search for riches and fame, subduing fire,
and steel, and heat, and cold. But I console
myself, in my humble state, to live content,
with the image of the lover I still desire
chiseled forever into my heart and soul.

---

Quando da bela vista e doce riso
tomando estão meus olhos mantimento,
tão enlevado sinto o pensamento
que me faz ver na terra o Paraíso.
Tanto do bem humano estou diviso,
que qualquer outro bem julgo por vento;
assi que em caso tal, segundo sento,
assaz de pouco faz quem perde o siso.
Em vos louver, Senhora, não me fundo,
porque, quem vossas cousas claro sente,
sentirá que não pode merecê-las.
Que de tanta estranheza sois ao mundo,
que não é de estranhar, Dama excelente,
que quem vos fez fizesse céu e estrelas.

## Paradise

Whenever your beautiful face and laughter entice
my hungry eyes, my mind is instantly swarmed
with thoughts that are so lofty and transformed,
I can see, right here on earth, God's Paradise.
Then I feel so isolated, so far above
mere human joys, which seem petty and unreal,
that I'm cut off from reality and feel
like someone who's lost his senses. Dear love,
my praise is always unworthy—as I am too,
like everyone else. I harbor no hopes to apprehend
your beauties, which only dazzle and mystify.
You're such a marvel in this world that seeing you,
Senhora, I'm never surprised to comprehend
that He who made you, made the stars and the sky.

*. . . santa Fénix, Virgem pura.*

---

Para se namorar do que criou
te fez Deus, santa Fénix, Virgem pura.
Vede que tal seria esta feitura
que a fez quem para si só a guardou.
No seu santo conceito te formou
primeiro que a primeira criatura,
para que única fosse a compostura
que de tão longo tempo se estudou.
Não sei se direi nisto quanto baste
para exprimir as santas qualidades
que quis criar em ti quem tu criaste.
És filha, mãe e esposa. E se alcançaste,
ũa só, três tão altas dignidades,
foi porque a três e um só tanto agradaste.

## The Virgin Mary

To fall in love with his whole world, his own
creation, God made you, most holy Mary,
a purest virgin so extraordinary
that God retained you for himself alone.
In his holy Mind, he conceived you, his paradigm,
long before Genesis, and long before Eve.
So we praise your singularity and believe
your essence was planned at the beginning of time.
I know that I could never, on my own,
fully express the holy qualities
created in you, who bore his perfect Son.
You're Daughter, Mother, and Wife. And if you alone
have exalted these three awesome dignities,
it's because you've delighted the Three-And-Only-One.

---

Dece do Céu imenso, Deus benino,
para encarnar na Virgem soberana.
«Porque dece divino em cousa humana?»
«Para subir o humano a ser Divino».
«Pois como vem tão pobre e tão minino,
rendendo-se ao poder da mão tirana?»
«Porque vem receber morte inumana
para pagar de Adão o desatino».
«Pois como? Adão e Eva o fruto comem
que por seu próprio Deus lhe foi vedado?»
«Si, por que o próprio ser de deuses tomem».
«E por essa razão foi humanado?»
«Si. Porque foi com causa decretado,
se o homem quis ser deus, que Deus seja homem».

# Incarnation

Descending from heaven, our most benign,
great God incarnated the Blessed Virgin. But why
did God descend to the human? To sanctify
all men, so they could aspire to the divine.
But why was he born so helpless and poor—to begin
His life under the tyrant, Herod? To prepare
the way for His sacrificial death, to bear
the penalties of Adam's foolish sin.
But Why? It was Adam and Eve who broke God's laws,
eating the forbidden fruits so long ago?
Yes, they tried to be "like gods" despite God's plan.
And that's why God became human? Yes, because,
in His mercy, He decided that, although
men wished to be gods, God would become Man.

---

Cara minha inimiga, em cuja mão
pôs meus contentamentos a ventura,
faltou-te a ti na terra sepultura,
por que me falte a mim consolação.
Eternamente as águas lograrão
a tua peregrina fermosura;
mas, enquanto me a mim a vida dura,
sempre viva em minha alma te acharão.
E se meus rudos versos podem tanto
que possam prometer-te longa história
daquele amor tão puro e verdadeiro,
celebrada serás sempre em meu canto;
porque enquanto no mundo houver memória,
será minha escritura teu letreiro.

## Drowned Lover

Dearest enemy, so often unkind,
my life was in your hands, until that wave
of the sea deprived you of an earthly grave,
depriving me, as well, of peace of mind.
The selfish drowning waters keep us apart,
enjoying your lovely beauty within the vast
cold sea, but as long as my broken life will last,
you'll always be alive within my heart.
And if my ragged poems can last for long
enough, your love, so spotless, will persist
forever and ever, as I, on your behalf,
will praise you always with my singing song;
as long as human memories exist,
my poems will be your missing epitaph.

*o grão Sebastião . . .*

---

Com o generoso rostro alanceado,
cheia de pó e sangue a real fronte,
chegou à triste barca de Aqueronte
o grão Sebastião, sombra tornado.
Vendo o cruel barqueiro que forçado
queria o rei passar, pôs-se defronte,
dizendo: «Pelas águas desta fonte,
nunca passou ninguém desenterrado».
O valoroso rei, com ira comovido,
lhe responde: «Ó falso velho, porventura
não passou outrem já com força d'ouro?
Pois a um rei banhado em sangue mouro
ousas tu perguntar por sepultura?
Pergunta-o a quem vier menos ferido».

## Sebastião

Smeared with flowing blood, with dust upon
his noble face, and pierced by the heathen's spear,
the shade of the great Sebastian, knowing no fear,
prepares to cross the deadly Acheron.
But the ancient boatman cries out loud,
blocking his path, standing face-to-face:
"Over the waters of this shadowy place,
the souls of the uninterred are *never* allowed."
Enraged, the king responds boldly and unafraid:
"Surely, old man, you won't deny that some
have passed your deceitful way with bribes of gold?
How dare you question a king, dead and unconsoled,
and drenched with Moorish blood! Mock those who come
without the open wounds of Christ's crusade."

---

Se a Fortuna inquieta e mal olhada,
que a justa lei do Céu consigo infama,
a vida quieta, que ela mais desama,
me concedera, honesta e repousada;
pudera ser que a Musa, alevantada
com luz de mais ardente e viva flama,
fizera ao Tejo lá na pátria cama
adormecer co som da lira amada.
Porém, pois o destino trabalhoso,
que me escurece a Musa fraca e lassa,
louvor de tanto preço não sustenta,
a vossa, de louvar-me pouco escassa,
outro sujeito busque valeroso,
tal qual em vós ao mundo se apresenta.

## To One Who's Praised Me

If fickle Fortune, with her evil eye
(always defaming the laws of Heaven), could
allow me something she detests: a good
and honest and peaceful life before I die,
my liberated Muse would suddenly leap
with fiery inspiration and deliver
such melodious songs they'd lull the river
Tagus, in lovely Portugal, to sleep.
But since my troubled destiny has been
inclined to enfeeble my Muse in countless ways,
your kindness seems undeserved and overly done.
So if you decide to offer such a tribute again,
seek out someone who's far more worthy of praise,
like yourself, whose worth is obvious to everyone.

---

Crecei, desejo meu, pois que a Ventura
já vos tem nos seus braços levantado;
que a bela causa de que sois gerado
o mais ditoso fim vos assegura.
Se aspirais por ousado a tanta altura,
não vos espante haver ao Sol chegado;
porque é de águia real vosso cuidado,
que, quanto mais o sofre, mais se apura.
Ânimo, coração! que o pensamento
te pode inda fazer mais glorioso,
sem que respeite a teu merecimento.
Que cresças inda mais é já forçoso,
porque, se foi de ousado o teu intento,
agora de atrevido é venturoso.

## Affirmation

Rise up, my aspirations, and ascend
to all your dreams! Good Fortune holds you in
her arms, shielding you from evil, within
and without, assuring you some glorious end.
Boldly aspire to even greater heights,
and don't be astonished if you soar to the sun
like the noble eagle who, in the long run,
grows more determined the more he struggles and fights.
Take courage, my Heart! All my thoughts affirm
your purpose; don't hesitate to boldly pursue
your dreams, regardless of social rank. Hold
to all your desires, and be strong and firm.
Be daring in everything you try to do,
and remember that Fortune smiles on the bold!

---

Dos Céus à terra dece a mór beleza,
une-se à carne nossa e fá-la nobre;
e, sendo a humanidade dantes pobre,
hoje subida fica à mór alteza.
Busca o Senhor mais rico a mór pobreza
que, como ao mundo o seu amor descobre,
de palhas vis o corpo tenro cobre,
e por elas o mesmo Céu despreza.
Como Deus em pobreza à terra dece?
O que é mais pobre tanto lhe contenta
que só rica a pobreza lhe parece.
Pobreza este Presépio representa.
Mas tanto, por ser pobre, já merece
que quanto é pobre mais, mais lhe contenta.

## Nativity Scene

The greatest beauty descends from heaven to earth,
uniting itself to our flesh and making it great
and noble. Once, it was humanity's fate
to be poor, but today it's exalted by His birth.
The richest Lord of all is satisfied
with the greatest poverty, sanctifying
his love for the world: a tender infant lying
in the straw, putting the glories of heaven aside.
Why did God come to earth so destitute?
Because he is content with what is poor,
since poverty is both precious and provident.
His birth, representing such absolute
destitution, reveals to us: that the more
the poverty, the more He is content.

---

Como podes, ó cego pecador,
estar em teus errores tão isento,
sabendo que esta vida é um momento,
se comparada com a eterna for?
Não cuides tu que o justo Julgador
deixará tuas culpas sem tormento,
nem que passando vai o tempo lento
do dia de horrendíssimo pavor.
Não gastes horas, dias, meses, anos,
em seguir de teus danos a amizade,
de que depois resultam mores danos.
E pois de teus enganos a verdade
conheces, deixa já tantos enganos,
pedindo a Deus perdão com humildade.

## Sermon

How, blind sinner, can you, so thoughtlessly,
commit these dreadful evils, always repeating
yourself, when you know that life is but a fleeting
moment in time compared with all eternity?
Never imagine that God, our Judge, will suspend
His laws and excuse your sins without their fair
just punishment—or that your day of despair
and reckoning will be slow to come. Don't spend
another hour, or day, or month, or year
befriending evils that will, in time, create
further damage and further retribution.
Since you know the truth of your errors, fear
them all, put them aside, and capitulate:
begging for God's mercy and absolution.

# Notes

*O dia em que eu naci moura e pereça . . .* / Curse (pages 24, 25)

See the Book of Job, Chapter 3.

*Enquanto quis Fortuna que tivesse . . .* / Reader (pages 28, 29)

Probably intended as the introductory sonnet for a collection that was never published. See Petrarch's "*Voi ch' ascoltate in rime sparse il suono . . .*"

*Brandas águas do Tejo que, passando . . .* / Tagus (pages 32, 33)

In the past, this sonnet was generally considered Camões's poetic adieu to the Tagus River as he sailed from Lisbon to India, but in modern times, this is a disputed attribution that some editors assign to the poet Diogo Bernardes.

*Por cima destas águas, forte e firme . . .* / Tears (pages 34, 35)

Traditionally, the subject of this sonnet has been assumed to be Camões's departure for India in 1553.

*Os vestidos Elisa revolvia . . .* / Dido (pages 36, 37)

See the *Aeneid,* Book IV, when Aeneas abandons his Carthaginian lover, Dido. The direct address to the sword by the despairing lover is unique to Camões. In the original, Camões uses Virgil's alternate name for Dido, "Elissa" (line 1), but I have used the more familiar Dido.

*Vós, Ninfas da gangética espessura . . .* / For Leonis Pereira (pages 38, 39)

Captain Leonis Pereira heroically defended the fortress of Malacca in modern Malaysia against an attack by the King of Achém. "Leónidas" (line 13) was the King of Sparta and the commander of the Greek forces against the Persians at Thermopylae, 480 BC. This is the only Camonian sonnet to be published in the poet's lifetime, appearing in Pêro de Magalhães Gândavo's *História da província de Santa Cruz a que vulgarmente chamam Brasil* (1576), a short history of Brazil.

*A fermosura desta fresca serra* . . . / Nature (pages 40, 41)

The location described in this beautiful nature poem is unclear. Despite "estranha terra" (line 5), the natural descriptions seem to imply Portugal, maybe Sintra, rather than the Orient.

*Quando o sol encoberto vai mostrando* . . . / On the Beach (pages 42, 43)

As elsewhere, Camões uses the term "inimiga" ("enemy," line 4) for his love.

*Amor é un fogo que arde sem se ver* . . . / Amor (pages 44, 45)

The paradoxical structure of this sonnet was common in Camões's time. See Petrarch' s "*Pace non trovo e non ò da far guerra* . . ."

*Todas as almas tristes se mostravam* . . . / Good Friday (pages 54, 55)

The widely believed tradition is that Camões first saw and fell in love with Caterina de Ataide, a young lady at the Lisbon court, during Good Friday Mass on April 13, 1544, in the Church of the Chagas. The similarities to Petrarch's first encounter with Laura are obvious, but they do not preclude the possibility of Camões's encounter. See Petrarch's "*Era il giorno ch' al soi si scoloraro* . . ."

*Quem jaz no grão sepulcro, que descreve* . . . / Sepulcher (pages 58, 59)

"Alexandre" (line 9) is Alexander the Great (356–323 BC). "Adriano" (line 11) is the Roman emperor Hadrian (76–138). "Numa" (line 13) is Numa Pompilius, the legendary successor to Romulus as the King of Rome, who presided over a golden age. "Joane / de Portugal terceiro" (lines 13, 14) is King João III (1502–57), known as "The Fortunate," who ruled the Portuguese empire from 1521 to 1557 when the young Camões was still attending court in Lisbon. This poem may have been written in response to the 1572 reinternment of King João's remains at the Monastery of Jerónimos in Belém.

*Ó gloriosa cruz, ó vitorioso* . . . / O Glorious Cross (pages 60, 61)

The poem might refer to the cross on the banner of King Sebastião. The last two lines of this sonnet are quite difficult, and their meaning is subject to debate.

*Um mover d'olhos, brando e piadoso . . .* / Magic (pages 62, 63)
"Circe" (line 13) is the powerful witch/goddess in Homer's *Odyssey,* Book X, who transforms Odysseus' sailors into swine. See Petrarch's "*Grazie ch' a pochi il Ciel largo destina . . .*"

*Na metade do Céu subido ardia . . .* / Natércia (pages 64, 65)
"Natércia" is an anagram for Caterina (Caterina de Ataide). "Eco" (line 14) is the chattering nymph, Echo, of Greek mythology whom Hera deprived of normal speech. When Echo fell in love with Narcissus, she was forced to entice him by repeating parts of his own speech, but this failed, and she was rejected, leading to Narcissus's punishment. Another Greek legend recounts that Echo was vainly loved by Pan, who drove the shepherds mad with his music until they tore her to pieces. "Liso" (line 9) is the shepherd's name and seemingly related to the poet's first name, Luís.

*No mundo, poucos anos e cansados . . .* / Pero Moniz (pages 66, 67)
Although a number of possibilities have been suggested, it seems most likely that this sonnet was dedicated to the memory of Pero Moniz, a young soldier who drowned in the Sea of Monte Felix off the coast of Africa. "Alenquer" (line 10), the apparent birthplace of Pero Moniz, is a small Portuguese town north of Lisbon. "Abássia" (line 13) is Abyssinia, modern-day Ethiopia, in Northeast Africa on the Red Sea. See Ovid's *Tristia* (I. 2) for "manjar de peixes" (line 12).

*Cá nesta Babilónia, donde mana . . .* / Exile (pages 72, 73)
Relates to the longing of the Jews for Jerusalem, "Sião" (line 14), during their captivity in "Babilónia" (line 1), as recorded in the Old Testament. For Camões, Babylon is Goa, and Jerusalem is Lisbon. Petrarch also used the Babylon/Zion analogy. "Mão" (line 4) is Venus.

*Debaixo desta pedra está metido . . .* / Dom Fernando (pages 76, 77)
Dom Fernando de Castro was a heroic Captain who died in the second attack at Diu, India (see *Os Lusíadas,* X, 70). "Viriato" (line 10) is Viriathus, the ancient leader of the Lusitani tribes who re-

volted against Rome in 147 BC and established an independent reign until his assassination in 139 BC. The difficult last tercet is considered a "true enigma" in Camonian scholarship.

*Doces águas e claras do Mondego . . .* / Mondego (pages 78, 79)

The Mondego River flows gently beneath the ancient capital town of Coimbra in north central Portugal, where the Universidade de Coimbra, which most scholars believe Camões attended, is located. Not referred to in the poem is the fact that Inês de Castro (see *Os Lusíadas,* III), the central figure in Portugal's greatest tragic romance, was murdered by King Afonso IV's henchmen on the banks of the Mondego in 1355. This sonnet has sometimes been published with a significant but poetically weaker variant in the last two tercets:

*Não quero de meus males outra glória*
*senão que lhe mostreis em vossas águas*
*as dos meus olhos, com que os seus se banhem.*

*Já pode ser que com minha memória,*
*vendo meus males, vendo minhas mágoas,*
*as suas com as minhas acompanhem.*

These tercets mean, rather literally:

*I do not want from my sorrows another glory,*
*(but) to show you in your waters,*
*the tears of my eyes, in which your (people) bathe.*

*It's possible that with my memory,*
*(and) looking at my sorrows, (and) looking at my grief,*
*(that) your (waters) with mine will mingle together.*

*Que modo tão sutil da Natureza . . .* / Escape (pages 80, 81)

This profession of the Franciscan habit might have taken place during the religious ceremony of 1572 presided over by the Lisbon Bishop António Pinheiro.

*"Que levas, cruel Morte?" "Um claro dia"* . . . / Dona Maria (pages 82, 83)
Several identities have been suggested for "Dona Maria" (line 8), including the Infanta Dona Maria who died in 1578, but the most likely candidate seems to be Dona Maria de Távora, who was a maid of honor to Queen Caterina.

*Senhor João Lopes, o meu baixo estado* . . . / Senhor João Lopes (pages 84, 85)
The poem is addressed to "Senhor João Lopes" (line 1), a contemporary of Camões in India and probably, like Camões, from a lower social station than his beloved.

*Orfeu enamorado que tañía* . . . / Orpheus (pages 86, 87)
One of thirty-five sonnets, many disputed, that Camões wrote in Spanish. It retells the myth of Orpheus, "Orfeu" (line 1), who tried unsuccessfully to rescue his dead wife Eurydice from hell. "Orco" (line 3) means "inferno" or "hell," coming from the infernal Greek deity Orcus, whom the Romans associated with Dis, and thus Pluto and Hades. "Ixión" (line 5) in Greek mythology was a Thessalian who murdered his father-in-law and then tried to seduce Hera. As punishment, Zeus placed him in hell bound to a wheel that rotates forever.

*Tornai essa brancura à alva açucena* . . . / Essence (pages 90, 91)
The "açucena" (line 1) is the Easter lily. The "Graças" (line 7) are the three Graces, the minor Greek goddesses of loveliness. The "serena" (line 8) are the Sirens who, in Homer and elsewhere, lure sailors to their doom with their irresistible song. The major female deities are represented in the sonnet by "Vénus," the goddess of beauty and love (line 9); "Minerva," the goddess of wisdom (line 10); and "Diana," the goddess of chastity (line 11).

*O cisne, quando sente ser chegada* . . . / Swan (pages 92, 93)
The last line is taken from the work of the Castilian poet Juan Boscán (1498?–1542), but the line no longer survives in the Castilian's extant poetry.

*Os reinos e os impérios poderosos* . . . / Dom Teodósio (pages 94, 95)
Dedicated to the successor of the House of Braganza, probably

the fifth duke (1532–63), although some scholars have made the claim for the seventh duke who did not actually succeed to the title until after Camões's death. Line 11 refers to Dom Teodósio's illustrious ancestors, King João I and Nuno Álvares Pereira, who secured Portuguese independence by defeating the Castilians in 1385. "Temístocles" (line 5) is the Athenian statesman Themistocles (525?–460? BC) who was responsible for the naval buildup and the strategy that defeated the Persians at the Battle of Salamis, 480 BC. The "Cipiões" (line 6) are the Scipios, the noble Roman family that produced Scipio Africanus Major (143?–183 BC), the conqueror of Hannibal in the Second Punic War, and Scipio Africanus Minor (185?–129 BC), the Roman general who destroyed Carthage (146 BC) at the end of the Third Punic War. Lines 7 and 8 refer to the exploits of the dozen Peers or Paladins of early France (see *Chanson de Roland*) and the Cids (see *Poema del Cid*) and the seven Laras of medieval Spain.

*Ilustre e dino ramo dos Meneses . . .* / Dom Fernando de Meneses (pages 96, 97) Dom Fernando de Meneses fought the Moors at Ceuta and later commanded a Red Sea expedition from India in 1553. "Eritreu" (line 7) is an Ethiopian province on the Red Sea; "Taprobana" is Ceylon; and Gedrosia" (line 11) is roughly Persia.

*Erros meus, má fortuna, amor ardente . . .* / Doom (pages 98, 99) Despite its difficult ending (lines 13–14), this is one of Camões's most famous and admired poems.

*Lindo e sutil traçado, que ficaste . . .* / Ribbon (pages 100, 101) The "trançado" (line 1) can refer to a number of hair adornments commonly worn by sophisticated Iberian women in the sixteenth century.

*Dizei, Senhora, da Beleza ideia . . .* / Perfection (pages 104, 105) "Medeia" (line 8) is the enchantress wife of Jason who, according to Euripides, kills her own children when Jason abandons her. "Narciso" (line 14) is the handsome youth Narcissus who spurned Echo (see *Na metade do Céu subido ardia . . .* / Natércia). When punished by Aphrodite, Narcissus becomes so enamored by his own reflection in a pool of water that he falls in and drowns.

*Enquanto Febo os montes acendia . . .* / Diana (pages 110, 111)

"Febo" (line 1) is the sun, identified with Phoebus Apollo. "Anquises" (line 6) is Anchises, a member of the royal house of Troy, who was seduced by Aphrodite (Venus). According to Virgil's *Aeneid,* he escaped from Troy, carried on the shoulders of his son, and wandered with Aeneas.

*Fiou-se o coração, de muito isento . . .* / Hippolytus (pages 112, 113)

"Hipólito" (line 9) is Hippolytus, the chaste son of King Theseus, who refused the incestuous seductions of his stepmother, Phaedra ("Fedra," line 10). Insulted, Phaedra convincingly told her husband that Hippolytus had tried to seduce her. In a rage, Theseus banished his son from Athens and left him to the wrath of Poseidon. When the sea-god frightened the young man from his chariot, Hippolytus was dragged to his death.

*Esforço grande, igual ao pensamento . . .* / Epitaph (pages 114, 115)

Dedicated to Dom Henrique de Meneses, who succeeded Vasco da Gama as the governor of India in 1524. See *Os Lusíadas,* X, 54. "Malabar" (line 8) is the coastal region of southwest India.

*Se os capitães antigos colocados . . .* / Conquistadors (pages 116, 117)

This homage to the accomplishments of the Portuguese heroes (see *Os Lusíadas,* I, 3) is dedicated to Dom Constantino de Bragança, the vice king of India.

*Tu que descanso buscas com cuidado . . .* / Refuge (pages 118, 119)

The attribution of this sonnet to the Camonian canon has been disputed.

*Alma minha gentil, que te partiste . . .* / Dear Gentle Soul (pages 126, 127)

The most famous and most translated of all Camões's sonnets. Inspired by Petrarch's "*Questa anima gentil che si disparte . . . ,*" tradition asserts that the poem was written when Camões learned of the death of Caterina de Ataide in 1556 when he was in Goa, India, possibly in jail. The poem has received much commentary, including chapter 10, "'Alma Minha Gentil' in English," in George Monteiro's *The Presence of Camões: Influences on the Literature of England, America, and Southern Africa* (Kentucky, 1996). Monteiro reprints nineteen English translations of the poem, from the anonymous version published in William Hayley's *An Essay on Epic Poetry; in Five Epistles* (1782) up to Monteiro's own rendering of 1994. I will cite three of the more enduring translations, all written by well-known poets, the first being the 1803 version by Robert Southey that was published in Lord Viscount Strangford's *Poems, from the Portuguese of Luis de Camoens; with Remarks on his Writings, Notes, &c.* (1803):

*Meek spirit, who so early didst depart,*
*Thou art at rest in heaven! I linger here*
*And feed the lonely anguish of my heart,*
*Thinking of all that made existence dear.*
*All lost! if in the happy world above,*
*Remembrance of this mortal life endure,*
*Thou wilt not there forget the perfect love*
*Which still thou seest in me, O spirit pure!*
*And if the irremediable grief,*
*The woe which never hopes on earth relief,*
*May merit aught of thee, prefer thy prayer*
*To God, who took thee early to his rest,*
*That it may please him soon amid the blest*
*To summon me, dear Maid! to meet thee there.*

In 1947, the most famous Portuguese poet of the twentieth century, Fernando Pessoa, who spent most of his youth in South Africa, also translated Camões's famous poem into English (appearing in *Translation,* Second Series, editors, Neville Graybrooke and Elizabeth King, Phoenix Press, London, 1947):

*Oh gentle spirit mine that didst depart*
*So early of this life in discontent,*
*With heavenly bliss thy rest be ever blest*
*While I on earth play wakeful my sad part.*
*If in the ethereal seat where now thou art*
*A memory of this life thou do consent,*
*Forget not that great love self-eloquent*
*Whose purity mine eyes here showed thy heart.*
*And, if thou see aught worthy of thy light*
*In the great darkness that hath come on me*
*From thine irreparable loss's spite,*
*Pray God, that made thy year so short to be,*
*As soon to haste me to thy deathless sight*
*As from my mortal sight he hasted thee.*

The distinguished South African poet Roy Campbell also translated the great Camonian sonnet, which was published in his posthumous book *Portugal* (Regnery, Chicago, 1958):

*Dear gentle soul, who went so soon away*
*Departing from this life in discontent,*
*Repose in that far sky to which you went*
*While on this earth I linger in dismay.*
*In the ethereal seat where you must be,*
*If you consent to memories of our sphere,*
*Recall the love which, burning pure and clear,*
*So often in my eyes you used to see!*
*If then, in the incurable, long anguish*
*Of having lost you, as I pine and languish,*
*You see some merit—do this favor for me:*
*And to the God who cut your life short, pray*
*That he as early to your sight restore me*
*As from my own he swept you far away.*

*Eu cantarei de amor tão docemente . . .* / Song of Love (pages 128, 129)
The first part of the sonnet follows Petrarch's "*Io canterei d'Amor sì novamente . . .*"

*Está o lascivo e doce passarinho . . .* / Little Bird (pages 132, 133)
"Estígio Lago" (line 8) is the Stygian lake or pond, also called the River Styx, which the dead must cross to enter into Hades. The "Frecheiro cego" (line 12) is Cupid, the blindfolded archer.

*Vencido está de Amor meu pensamento . . .* / For Caterina (pages 136, 137)
This amazing tour de force is a double-acrostic sonnet, traditionally assumed to have been written for Caterina de Ataide. The initial letters of the fourteen lines spell out, "voso como cati[j]vo," meaning literally, "yours as captive." In their place, I have used, in English, "I am your captive." The initial letters of the seventh metrical syllable in each of Camões's lines spell out, "mu[v]i alta senhora," meaning literally, "most high lady." I have used, in my English version, "My peerless love."

*Quando de minhas mágoas a comprida . . .* / Dinamene (pages 138, 139)
"Dinamene" (lines 12, 13) was the nymph daughter of the sea-god Nereus and the Oceanid Doris. She is mentioned in Homer and Hesiod, and also in Garcilaso de la Vega. Many Camonian scholars have assumed that the identity of "Dinamene," to whom the poet refers in a number of his poems, was a native lover, possibly Chinese, with whom Camões lived in the Orient, and who drowned in the terrible shipwreck off Cambodia in 1559.

*Na ribeira do Eufrates assentado . . .* / Euphrates (pages 140, 141)
"Eufrates" (line 1) is the River Euphrates that flows through Babylon (Goa), and "Sião" (line 4) is Jerusalem, and thus Lisbon. See *Cá nesta Babilónia, donde mana . . .* / Exile (pages 72, 73) and its note.

*Aquela que, de pura castidade . . .* / Lucretia (pages 142, 143)
This poem refers to the Roman legend of Lucretia, the wife of Tarquinius Collatinus, who stabbed herself to death after being raped by Sextus, the son of King Tarquinius Superbus of Rome. The outrage over this crime and Lucretia's subsequent suicide lead to an

insurrection that expelled the Tarquins from power. See Chaucer's *The Legend of Good Women* and Shakespeare's *The Rape of Lucrece.*

*Que vençais no Oriente tantos reis . . .* / Luís de Ataíde (pages 144, 145)

This poem is addressed to Luís de Ataíde who served as Governor of India from 1568 to 1571 and returned as vice governor in 1577.

*Sete anos de pastor Jacob servia . . .* / Jacob (pages 146, 147)

See Genesis 29, which relates the love of Jacob for Rachel and the duplicity of her father, Laban.

*Debaixo desta pedra sepultada . . .* / Caterina (pages 148, 149)

Many Camonian scholars feel that this epitaph for a beloved young woman was written for Caterina de Ataide, but it is impossible to be certain.

*O céu, a terra, o vento sossegado . . .* / The Wind (pages 150, 151)

"Aónio" (line 5), the name of the fisherman, is a confusing and much-debated anagram for the female name "Ioana" or "Joana."

*Em prisões baixas fui um tempo atado . . .* / Prison (pages 152, 153)

This powerful and well-known sonnet relates to Camões's incarcerations in Lisbon and Goa.

*Para se namorar do que criou . . .* / The Virgin Mary (pages 160, 161)

"És filha, mãe e esposa" (line 12) refers Mary to the doctrine of the Holy Trinity, the "três e um" referred to in line 14. This poem has sometimes been attributed to Diogo Bernardes and others.

*Dece do Céu imenso, Deus benino . . .* / Incarnation (pages 162, 163)

The "tirana" (line 6) is Herod Antipas, the cruel Tetrarch of Galilee from 4 BC to 39 AD, referred to in Matthew, Mark, Luke, and Acts. Line 11 refers to Adam and Eve's wish to "be as gods," Genesis 3:5.

*Cara minha inimiga, em cuja mão . . .* / Drowned Lover (pages 164, 165)

This sonnet is traditionally assumed to be about the poet's drowned lover in the Orient, Dinamene. See *Quando de minhas mágoas a comprida . . .* / Dinamene (pages 138, 139) and its note.

*Com o generoso rostro alanceado . . .* / Sebastião (pages 168, 169)

This famous memorial poem, of somewhat disputed authorship, refers to the death of King Sebastião of Portugal in the disastrous

Moroccan battle of Alcàcer-Kebir in 1578, two years before the death of the poet in Lisbon. Previously, in 1572, Camões had dedicated his *Os Lusíadas* to the young monarch. "Aqueronte" (line 3) is Acheron, one of the rivers in Hades, and "o cruel barqueiro" (line 5) is Charon, the ferryman, who transports the dead over the infernal waters to Hades. Charon is mentioned in both Virgil's *Aeneid,* Book IV, and Dante's *Inferno,* Canto III.

# Selected Bibliography

The most useful modern editions of the lyrics are Maria de Lurdes Saraiva's well-annotated *Luís de Camões Lírica Completa, Sonetos,* Volume Two (1980), and Cleonice Serôa da Motta Berandinelli's *Sonetos de Camões: corpus dos sonetos Camonianos* (1980). The best English language translations of selected sonnets, both out of print, are Jonathan Griffin's fourteen sonnets in *Camões: Some Poems* (1976) and Keith Bosley's twenty sonnets included in L. C. Taylor's *Luís de Camões: Epic and Lyric* (1990). Although the two significant nineteenth century translations of the sonnets are quite antiquated and syntactically awkward for modern readers (Keith Bosley refers to Burton's translations as a "monument to unreadability"), both are still useful and often instructive. They are, as previously cited in the introduction, J. J. Aubertin's *Seventy Sonnets of Camoens* (1881) and Sir Richard Burton *Lyricks of Camoens* (1884).

The best biography of the poet is the German scholar Friedrich Wilhelm Storck's *Luis de Camoens Leben* (1890), while the introduction to Antônio Salgado's *Obra Completa* (1963) contains much updated and useful information about the countless mythologies surrounding Camões's remarkable life. In English, the short and outdated biography of Aubrey F. G. Bell, *Luiz de Camões* (1923), is still useful, whereas Henry H. Hart's overly speculative *Luis de Camoëns and the Epic of the Lusiads* (1962) is less so. Regarding *Os Lusíadas,* the original Sir Richard Fanshawe translation (1655) is still excellent reading, but there have been a number of more recent and very successful renderings of the great classic. Two recommended versions that are still in print are Leonard Bacon's *The Lusiads of Luis de Camões* (1950) and Langdeg White's *The Lusíads* (1997).

Regarding critical study on the sonnets, the early commentaries of

Manuel de Faria e Sousa in his 1685 edition of *Rimas Várias* are indispensible. Sir Richard Burton's appendix to his *Lyricks* of 1884 is still quite useful, but a more serious analysis of the sonnets and the important question of debatable attribution was begun by Storck's aforementioned biography in 1890 and has continued throughout the twentieth century. Especially important are: Jorge de Sena's *Os sonetos de Camões e o soneto quinhentista peninsular* (1969); Cleonice Berardinelli's annotated edition of the *Sonetos de Camões: corpus dos sonetos camonianos* (1980); Leodegário A. de Azevedo Filho's *Introdução à lírica de Camões* (1991); Marina Machado Rodrigues' discussion of authorship, "Crítica autoral e crítica textual na Lírica de Camões dois problemas," in *Revista Camoniana,* Série 2, volume 10, 1997; and Helen Vendler's "Camões the Sonneteer" in *Portuguese Literary and Cultural Studies,* No. 9, 2002.

# Acknowledgments

Certain translations in this collection have been previously published in the following journals: "Exile," "Sepulcher," and "Jacob" in *Modern Poetry in Translation;* "Curse" and "Tagus" in *Acumen;* "Refuge," "Good Friday," "Epitaph," "Dear Gentle Soul," "Pero Moniz," "Dinamente," "Sin," "Dead Lovers," "Drowned Lover," "Dawn," "Natércia," and "Shipwreck" in *First Things;* "Mondego," "Cruel Senhora," "Hippolytus," "Doom," "Time," "Dona Maria," and "Essence" in *Portuguese Literary and Cultural Studies;* "The Wind" in *Saint Ann's Review;* and "O Glorious Cross," "Nativity Scene," and "Incarnation" in *The Wanderer.*

# Index of Titles and First Lines